Confessions of a Transformed Heart
Youth Edition

with Discussion Questions

Nancy D. Sheppard

© 2013 Nancy D. Sheppard

Cover photo and art by Heidi Sheppard

The names of certain persons mentioned in this book have been changed in order to protect the privacy of the individuals involved.

CONFESSIONS OF A TRANSFORMED HEART – Youth Edition (with Discussion Questions)

Copyright © 2013 by Nancy Sheppard

First Edition © 2010 by Nancy D. Sheppard

All rights reserved. This book or any portion thereof may not be reproduced or used in any manner whatsoever without the express written permission of the publisher except for the use of brief quotations in a book review. For questions regarding copyright permission please contact the author at Confessions@sheppardsmissions.org

Scripture is taken from the New King James Version®. Copyright © 1982 by Thomas Nelson, Inc. Used by permission. All rights reserved.

Confessions of a Transformed Heart –Youth Edition is available in paperback, as a Kindle book and as an audio book.

See http://www.sheppards-books.com

Published by Sheppard's Books, USA

> Non-fiction missionary story
> History of Liberian conflict
> ISBN: 978-1-940172-04-0
> Sheppard, Nancy, 1960-

Dedicated to Mark,
John-Mark, Melodie,
Nathan, Heidi,
Jared and Jonah

Contents

Prologue 1
Chapter 1: In the Beginning 3
Chapter 2: Liberia, Here We Come! 13
Chapter 3: Rice Riot 21
Chapter 4: An Uncivil War 25
Chapter 5: Refugees 33
Chapter 6: The Confrontation 45
Chapter 7: Heidi 57
Chapter 8: Surprised by the Power of Prayer 61
Chapter 9: The Emptying 69
Chapter 10: In Love 81
Chapter 11: Good News 85
Chapter 12: Patience 91
Chapter 13: Mom 97
Chapter 14: The Making of a Man 103
Chapter 15: Becoming Sarah's Daughter 111
Chapter 16: Tested by Fire 115
Chapter 17: Back at Last 121
Chapter 18: The Trap Closes 125
Chapter 19: The Upgrades 129
Chapter 20: Foolish Things 135
Chapter 21: Merri 141
Chapter 22: Grabbing Grace 149
Chapter 23: Mouse Poison 153
Chapter 24: Preston 157
Epilogue 169
Appendix 1: Intercessory Prayer Requests for Liberia ... 175
Appendix 2: How to be Changed from the Inside Out ... 177
Appendix 3: Adoption 183
Appendix 4: Discussion Questions 189
Bibliography 197

Prologue

"If you feel you *can't* go back, we won't. But if you simply don't want to, we will. So which is it?"

Rather than the expected relief—finally, finally, *finally* I could get out of my awful predicament—in the dead silence as my husband awaited my response I realized, unbelievably, my future as well as the future of my entire family hinged on my next sentence.

Indeed, I was in a very serious bind. As American missionaries to Liberia, for the last year we'd lived in its neighboring country, the Ivory Coast, working among the refugees of what was becoming one of Africa's most brutal civil wars. And it was awful.

Contrary to popular assumption, meaningful work among the impoverished and war torn was *not* romantic, but was in fact quite the opposite. War refugees were simply people. People ripped from their homes, material goods and every vestige of normal life. Humanity at its rawest—all props gone. All of my props were gone too. In place of the chipper, Proverbs 31 wife I had imagined myself to be was a miserable, depressed, nagging shadow.

Living among thousands of war refugees was not what I had in mind when I volunteered for missionary service ten years earlier. I was a planner by nature, and neither my life plan, nor my ten year, five year, yearly, weekly, nor daily plans included working with insatiably needy people who were not only insufficiently grateful I was there, they actually made a sport of finding fault. These people didn't deserve me!

Could a God of love ask me to live in a place where I was in such abject misery? Surely not! How had I, a girl from Whitewater, Wisconsin, ended up in that God-forsaken corner of the earth anyway?

Chapter 1: In the Beginning

Noticeably blessed from the moment of conception—I have an identical twin sister—it never seriously crossed my mind God would ask something really, really difficult of me.

Nancy and Karen Brushaber as babies

My parents, Melvin and Ellen Brushaber, raised my three brothers, my sister and me in a renovated summerhouse next to a charming lake. Warm, lazy summers were filled with swimming and toasting our winter-white skin to a golden brown on well-worn beach towels. Autumn's crisp days meant school, music lessons and friends. Winter's highlight was Christmas with all its magic. Surrounded by a large extended family, Grandma would set the traditional baked goose in the center of the table amid a bounty of steaming dishes. Aunt Shirley read the Christmas story from the Bible while Danish rice pudding boiled in the kitchen.

Spring brought Easter with its special dresses and church services. Summer, fall, winter, and spring—I loved it all.

"When you pray, you mean it," a friend at my Christian university told me. And I did. God had been very real to me from the moment Christ took residence in my heart as a five-year-old little girl. God provided Jesus, His Son, as a sacrifice so my sins could be forgiven, my mom had explained. Jesus died that horrible death on the cross for *me*. That night Karen and I were born into God's family through faith in Jesus Christ as Savior from sin, becoming twins a second time.

With a strong emphasis on Christian service in my home and then in the Christian high school and college I attended, my entire childhood and youth were spent pursuing absolutely every program or activity the church had to offer. My family was the first to arrive (we had the key!) and often the last to leave. I attended AWANA and won awards for Bible verse memorization. As I reached junior and then senior high school, I played the piano for services and was faithful to the busy youth group program. Extremely conscious of what others thought of me, I steered clear of anything close to real trouble. I wanted God's will for my life and told Him so regularly. From a young age I knew God wanted me in full-time Christian service. Whatever. Wherever. I was the quintessential Baptist "good girl."

Although a Baptist, Mark Sheppard was not the quintessential good boy. Nevertheless, when our paths crossed at the Christian University we both attended, we hit it off right away and became good friends. Mark had an irrepressible sense of humor that I loved. He was a prankster and a goofball who'd spent regular time in the principal's office as a kid. He regaled me for hours with tales of broken bones, misadventures and exploits past and present. Mark was an excellent student, which I admired, and, unlike me, he questioned things. I found Mark fascinating.

While we were opposite in many ways, we shared a commonality more important than any difference. We both truly loved the Lord and wanted what He wanted for our lives. There was no romantic pressure whatsoever on our relationship because

In the Beginning

Mark was planning to marry my friend, who was sitting out the semester. So with innocence we laughed and played together, knowing this was temporary. When Mark's girlfriend returned their relationship officially ended. Eventually our friendship turned to love and I realized it was meant to be something more. Mark Sheppard was God's choice for me.

Mark was anything but the boring, serious person I assumed I would marry. (After all, I wanted to serve God and that was deadly serious business!) I wish I had ten dollars for every person who warned me marrying Mark was a risk I surely didn't realize I was taking. Their dire warnings confirmed one thing; Mark needed me. "Miss Good Girl" would help "Mr. Intellectual Goofball" become the God-fearing man he was meant to be. He was so blessed to get me.

In Whitewater, Wisconsin on June 21, 1980, on an absolutely perfect summer day, Mark and I were married. My face hurt from smiling. *Lord, Send Me Anywhere,* with word changes making all singular pronouns plural, was beautifully sung. I had no idea God would take us so seriously.

<u>Lord, Send Me Anywhere</u>
O Lord, since Thou hast died
To give Thyself for me,
No sacrifice could be too great
For me to make for Thee.

I only have one life,

And that will soon be past;
I want my life to count for Christ,
What's done for Him will last.

I follow Thee, my Lord,
And glory in Thy cross;
I gladly leave the world behind
And count all gain as loss.

Chorus:
Lord, send me anywhere, Only go with me;
Lay any burden on me, Only sustain me.
Sever any tie, Save the tie that binds me to Thy heart;
Lord Jesus, my King, I consecrate my life, Lord, to Thee.[1]

Nancy's 1981 graduation from Bob Jones University

I finished up my Home Economics Education degree our first year of marriage. During that time Mark, a graduate in Broadcast Engineering, sent his résumé to Christian radio ministries across the U.S. He was perplexed when he received no replies. Apparently during the time of his university education the boom in the

---

[1] David Livingstone and Faye Springer Lopez, "Lord, Send Me Anywhere," Greenville, SC, Musical Ministries / Majesty Music, 1978.

In the Beginning

Christian radio market had ended. With no job opening in his field, there was little we could do after my college graduation but return to Minneapolis, Mark's home town, and await God's leading.

Mark, talented in all things electronic, wired houses and businesses while I taught English, Bible and home economics at a Christian school. However, as the school year progressed we were plagued with frustration. We were doing well financially, but surely God had something more for us than this nine-to-five existence. But what?

In February of 1982 our church, Valley Baptist of Golden Valley, Minnesota, held a weeklong conference featuring Dr. Allan Lewis, a godly man with a heart beating for world missions. He was the president of Baptist Mid-Missions, an independent Baptist agency representing more than 1100 missionaries scattered across the globe. One evening he mentioned a radio ministry in Italy. Our ears perked up.

We talked with Dr. Lewis privately and it was most enlightening. While missionaries in Italy were using radio to spread the gospel and it was a great ministry opportunity, he also knew of another possibility. Baptist Mid-Missions' missionaries in Liberia wanted to broadcast Bible teaching in tribal languages. They needed someone technically proficient to set up and run a radio station in the interior of the country. With Mark's educational background, Dr. Lewis felt he could be the perfect man for the job. Sensing God was leading in that direction, we applied to the mission and were accepted in July of 1982.

We were intrigued by Liberia's unique history, of which we knew precious little before our decision to go there. Unlike any other country in the entire world, Liberia's history was intimately tied to the history of the United States, making it our history as well as theirs.

In the early 1800's, several decades before America's bloody Civil War, a perplexing series of questions began to dominate conversations at dinner tables, pubs and political gatherings. Not surprisingly, given the deep division over the subject, they were about slavery.

At this point in time few people thought abolition even a possibility. The vast majority of black-skinned Americans were in slavery, enjoying no freedom and no civil rights. They were property. But, and here was the dilemma, there was an ever-growing group of people who were black and free—having become so by either buying their freedom or having been set free by a master. What should be done with them? Some believed that because of their skin color and heritage, freed slaves had no right to expect equal standing before the law. Others felt it was unlikely the freed slaves would ever be able to successfully integrate into U.S. society. An ever-growing group of concerned Americans felt repatriation to their African homeland was the obvious solution to the dilemma.

In 1816 the American Colonization Society, the A.C.S., was formed. Its all-white associates were motivated by reasons as varied as prejudice, fear and philanthropy. Nevertheless, they worked together and after a lot of planning, recruiting and hard work, in 1820 eighty-eight former slaves, accompanied by three A.C.S. members, set sail for the coastline of Africa.

Not surprisingly, things didn't go smoothly. Unable to find anyone willing to sell them land, the would-be colonists were forced to take shelter on a small island off Sierra Leone. Many died of malaria or one of the other diseases that lurked in the new-to-them tropical climate. Finally, after many months, a local ruler was coerced into selling a strip of land to the society.

A mixed lot joined these initial settlers in the years following. Included were newly freed slaves (some freed only on the condition they return to Africa), those who had been born free and those from seized slaving ships whose human cargo had been declared illegal.

The new colony, named Liberia, took as its motto, "The love of liberty brought us here." Monrovia, the capital city, was named after James Monroe, the fifth president of the United States and an avid supporter of the project.

In the Beginning

Obviously the new settlers had never lived a day in Africa. In fact, as soon as they landed they realized they weren't Africans at all. They were Americans. They spoke, thought, lived, dressed and survived in a way distinctly different than the locals. Many of the new colonists had a noticeable amount of white ancestry and didn't even look like the locals.

Having no model other than the one they knew from personal experience, the colonists patterned their lives and relationships with the indigenous people after the model of a Southern slave owner. Some found no irony in enslaving the local population. And unlike an African slave in the southern United States, a slave of this new and up-coming elite group of people was a very easily and very cheaply replaced commodity.

Even with the exploitation of the indigenous people, the task of carving a new life for themselves in this new place was far from easy for the new colonists. Each year torrential rains poured down for months on end, ruining goods that were irreplaceable except by import. Diseases to which their bodies had no natural resistance were a daily threat. And nothing about being freed slaves prepared them to settle in a new land among people of whose tribal languages and customs they were completely ignorant.

Nevertheless, the settlers prospered financially. Lavish houses surrounded by wide verandahs were built. Their homes and clothing, complete with gloved hands and lacy parasols, reflected their Southern past.

Society members as well as the freed slaves assumed Christianity would be brought to the local population as the result of this reintegration into Africa. Beautiful churches, complete with stained glass and bells, were built. However, instead of converting the tribal people from spiritism to Christianity, the coastal "Americo-Liberians," as they were called, added the tribal people's spiritism to the mixture of traditional Christianity and spiritism they had embraced before their reintegration to Africa. At the same time the tribal people wedded their traditional spiritism with this new spiritistic/Christian blend.

Liberia, about the size of the state of Tennessee, became an independent nation in 1848. Its constitution was patterned after that of the U.S. Its flag's blue field with a lone star on top of red and white stripes was patterned after Old Glory.

Americo-Liberians were the ruling class of the newly formed country. The True Whig political party, controlled by the Americo-Liberians, represented less than five percent of the population but, nevertheless, ruled for more than one hundred years straight—often with unchallenged corruption, discrimination and nepotism. The "savages" or "aborigines," as they called them, were second-class citizens and their concerns largely unaddressed.

This continued until 1980 when Master Sergeant Samuel Doe, along with sixteen enlisted men of the Armed Forces, murdered Liberia's last True Whig President, William Tolbert. Doe declared himself president and the country, at least on the surface, accepted him as just that. He was the first Liberian president who could make no claim of an ancestry harking back to U.S. slavery days.

In the Beginning

It was to this Liberia we felt God was calling us. Baptist Mid-Missions, named for its willingness to reach into the "mid" and often unreached portion of African countries, began its work there in 1938. Before there were roads, much less maps marking them, dedicated American missionaries walked into the interior and settled on properties granted by the Liberian government. Despite unimaginable hardships, dangerous tropical diseases and the very real possibility of death to precious children, these dedicated men and women followed where God led. Their "church planting" efforts had been extremely successful. Scattered throughout the country were several hundred churches and fellowships that had been started by either missionaries or the Liberian men they had trained.

Now, almost fifty years later, Mark and I planned to follow in the footsteps of those pioneers. We knew we looked pathetically young to those to whom we presented our ministry plans. "Trust us. We know what we're doing," we joked with each other. We also joked, "Let's tell our 'Life of Sin' testimonies tonight." Our lack of a notably sinful past felt boring and totally forgettable so we invented more interesting "testimonies" as we traveled. Needless to say, we always controlled ourselves and told our real stories from the pulpit. Imperfect though we knew ourselves to be, we knew God had people much more seriously flawed than us on whom to concentrate.

Chapter 2: Liberia, Here We Come!

On April 14, 1986, at 29 and 26 years of age, Mark and I stepped out of the air-conditioned comfort of KLM's Boeing 747 into Liberia's tropical heat. We were in Africa at last! Below us the tarmac steamed in the early evening light. Mark held John-Mark, age three, by the hand while I carried Melodie, age one. Another baby was expected in July.

As the van sped from the airport I stared out the opened windows. Every imaginable shade of green produced a verdant beauty for which nothing in my mid-western background prepared me. Palm trees pointed to the stars as dusk turned to darkness. Approaching the city, I breathed in the humid, spicy air. Our driver wove through incredibly noisy traffic as thousands of pedestrians darted in all directions.

At the mission's guest compound new missionary friends hugged Mark and me warmly. Brown-skinned Liberians grabbed our hands and shook them in the traditional manner—a snap produced with the thumbs and middle fingers as the two hands separate. "Thank you for coming," they exuded. They'd prayed for us. They'd waited for us. They were so excited about the prospect of this new radio station.

The next day began the baptism into Liberian English. "How da' body?" sounded shockingly intimate, but I soon realized it was standard. "Fine-o." Mastering the Liberian "o" was important. If sick or having an especially difficult day, "Tryin'," or "Tryin' small," was the correct response. There was the repeated word for emphasis. "Small-small" (very small) and "big-big" (very big). And while I was pathetically inept at making sense of the English that lay under the thick Liberian accent, at least it wasn't Swahili.

After six weeks in Monrovia, missionary Chick Watkins flew us in the mission's six-passenger Cessna to Tappita. In the back seat with John-Mark and Melodie my heart filled with awe. We passed winding rivers beside mountains rich in iron ore. Gigantic trees in the lush rain forest looked like broccoli stalks from my aerial view. These jungles were home to rare chimpanzees, dwarf elephants, forest buffalo, duikers, leopards, pigmy hippos, ibis, eagles, hornbills, hawks and hundreds more unique and exotic animals.

Tappita was a small interior town of several thousand people—the mission station property located at its edge atop a large hill. Our mud-brick house stood serenely on a beautiful green yard, surrounded by fourteen mango trees. Cashews with their little "apples," pink grapefruit and green-yellow oranges hung from trees lining the yard. A flock of African Gray parrots passed overhead each evening, squawking noisily. With the birth of Nathan on July 19, we were a family of five living an amazing adventure in Africa.

It was exciting for us rookies to work together with the nine veteran missionaries already living in Tappita. The commonality of our goals and close proximity of our houses pushed us together emotionally and physically. Although we admired each one, Chick Watkins' obvious love of God and the Liberian people, as well as his infectious enthusiasm and boundless vision for the future, set him apart. We admired Chick and Joan for raising six godly children and for their more than twenty-five years of missionary service in Liberia. We wanted to be just like them.

Our missionary team was busy in a number of important ministries. Many days I heard one of the airplanes rev up and then rumble down the grassy airstrip. In the evening it returned, completing yet another successful evangelistic or humanitarian flight. The mission property hummed with busy Bible school students. With three levels of education available, there was something for everyone—from those who had never been to school before to those who were high school graduates. The sick made their way to the mission's clinic for the quality care it offered at bargain prices. Tuesday's "belly day" brought in dozens of ladies for prenatal checkups, their bulging tummies wrapped in bright lappa cloth.

Mark and Chick Watkins with a Bible school graduate

Mark loved the challenge of setting up a radio station in the middle of the jungle. The project was huge and very physical. He and every willing man kept busy as power lines were constructed, the tower site cleared, the tower erected and electronic equipment installed. Mark was so in his element he actually bemoaned the day the project would be completed and the radio station on the air. He was having fun!

Because we lived on the same property as the Bible school and clinic, everything was within easy walking distance. This made it possible for me to be involved in several ministries even though I had three small children. I shared the gospel with clinic patients recovering from childbirth. I cared for visitors coming to help with the radio station and took my turn as mission station hostess. Besides helping other missionary wives by sharing in the teaching of their children, I also taught Bible studies, English and home economics to Liberians of a variety of ages and educational levels.

Each Wednesday I walked down the deeply rutted roads into market to enjoy the best "flea market" ever. The goods—dried  and fresh meats, mountains of rice, canned tomato paste, bouillon cubes, pots, plastic dishes, soap, African cloth, and a delightful assortment of garden produce—were displayed on rickety tables. On the ground mounds of wrinkled used clothing from the U.S. were heaped on clear sheets of plastic. The market bustled with buyers and sellers. Noisy, enthusiastic shoppers greeted friends and tended to squalling children. Voices ricocheting across the outdoor market created a noisy sense of community I found enchanting.

Our social life was interesting and varied. Picturesque outdoor feasts with the Bible school students and their families boasted rugged, wooden tables weighed down with huge pots of steaming rice and smaller pots of Liberian soup. The chop suey-like mixture of meat ("cow meat," "pig meat" or "chicken meat"), vegetables, oil and bouillon cubes was quite delicious, though strange-looking to our American eyes. The missionary team worked hard, but we also played hard. Skits, songs, Rook tournaments, a Valentine's Day party (Mark and I acted out a ridiculous "Harlequin Romance" I wrote for the occasion), and Christmas dinner together in a screened-in pavilion created wonderfully-fun breaks from the hard but fulfilling work.

Never a country girl, I was intrigued by the simple pleasure of eating a grapefruit plucked from a tree in our own yard or a pineapple I'd watched grow and then ripen to succulent sweetness. It was fascinating to watch chicks grow from hatchlings to gangly adolescents to crowing, table-ready, adult roosters. Mark was given several hens and roosters as gifts from grateful church

Liberia, Here We Come!

members and they became temporary and welcome, albeit noisy and smelly, members of the family. We gave them silly names—Miss Marple, Agatha Christie and Lucky, to name a few. Lucky wasn't actually his original name, but rather an earned title. After multiple failed attempts to kill him and cook him up for dinner, no other name would do.

Our small children thrived in their outdoor, summer-all-year-'round life. Exotic pets weren't exotic to them. Our mongoose Rikki-tikki-tavi, named after the mongoose made famous by Rudyard Kipling in *The Jungle Book*, ran to baby Nathan who was sitting on the tiled floor. Over and over Nathan picked him up and tossed him. Rikki came back for more. Nathan laughed, thoroughly delighted. Annie, the Watkins' baby chimp, came by to visit from time to time, making great "photo ops" as she grabbed Melodie's hand and walked beside her. John-Mark roamed the edge of the jungle outside our house, slingshot in hand, hunting for lizards. At night the children fell asleep to a symphony of insects, distant tree bear[1] calls, and the rustle of jungle leaves.

It was thrilling to get to know a totally different culture than the one in which I'd grown up. While I enjoyed "people watching" in general, the women especially fascinated me. I could easily see we shared a number of commonalities, but I couldn't help notice the many differences between us as well. My blond hair and fair skin contrasted sharply with my Liberian counterpart's black cornrows and rich, chocolate-brown skin. My physical weakness stood at variance with the almost brute strength I observed. Ladies balanced heavy loads on their heads, sometimes while toting babies on their backs. Lacking any of the modern conveniences that I'd grown up taking for granted, these women hand-washed clothes in creeks, rivers or lagoons or with water drawn from an open well. Rather than shopping for food at a grocery store, the women cooked and ate the food they'd grown in their gardens and "slash and burn"-style farms. And most glaringly, I had enjoyed educational opportunities of which they dared not even dream.

Each January our interior mission station hosted a seminar for the women of the Mano and Gio tribes. The two weeks were filled with singing, teaching and preaching. My first year in Liberia, as I taught principles for Christian living in the home to the large group, I was extremely conscious of how different my life was from the lives of those who sat before me. I felt so young, so rich, and so white. I wanted the cultural barriers to fall down and for them to know and understand me. I wanted to know and understand them as well.

For months I'd been hearing about the seminar's amazing party night and I wondered if this would be my chance to connect with the women on a more personal level. Upon arrival at the much-acclaimed event, Kool-Aid and cookies in hand, I watched dust rise to the ceiling in cloudy puffs of brown as the ladies played a game they called Snake. Setting down the re-

---

[1] Tree hyrax

freshments, I jumped in, sure it must be easier than it looked. It wasn't. In fact, it was much harder than it looked. After a few minutes I sat down, completely overwhelmed.

There followed an exhausting series of games, all involving complicated foot movements—often in unison. I was amazed at the strength and coordination of even the oldest women. How did they know when to jump and which foot to use? I couldn't even begin to figure out the intricacies of the games they played so effortlessly. I left the party feeling every bit the newbie—and not particularly enjoying it.

In the year following that first seminar, Liberia became my home in a way I never dreamed possible. I found it exciting and perhaps even a bit heady to be living a life that was so unique. I loved my quaint, mud-brick house in its park-like yard. I loved the warm, tropical weather. I had several missionary friends to whom I felt particularly close and I was connecting more and more with the Liberian women.

As my second seminar approached I was not nearly as nervous as I'd been the year before. I was confident the material I'd prepared would challenge the ladies and be quite fun for me to teach as well. And although intimidated by even the thought of playing the games I'd for the most part only watched, I determined that this year I'd participate in every one.

By the time I arrived with my refreshments in hand for Thursday night's party, the atmosphere was already electric. Brown eyes sparkled with excitement when the first game was introduced. Sandaled feet began stomping. Strong hands began clapping. I stepped into the circle of laughing women, knowing I needed to get in quickly or I'd lose my nerve. Dark hands grabbed me from each direction. I looked down at their fast-moving feet and jumped, attempting to copy what I was seeing. No success. I tried again. Hilarious laughter followed each move I made. The worse I played the game, the harder they laughed. I looked into their eyes: they weren't laughing *at* me, they were laughing *with* me. It was obvious to them that now I was the student and they the teachers. And they loved it!

The party was a success for everyone. I was predictably terrible at every game. Each failure brought the laughter reserved for friends who are known and loved—the laughter of acceptance and camaraderie.

In 1989 we returned to the U.S. tanned and joyful with our three beautiful children for our one-year home assignment. We were young, vital and involved in something important. Our first three-year term in missionary service had been everything we dared hope, plus some. I loved God and was surrendered to His will. (I was, after all, a missionary to Africa.) I knew my life would be wonderful. It already *was* wonderful. Everything was exactly as it should be.

Nancy, Nathan, Melodie, Mark, John-Mark in front of the radio station building—1989

Chapter 3: Rice Riot

While we were celebrating a traditional Danish Christmas in Whitewater, Wisconsin with my extended family, blissfully ignorant of what was happening on the other side of the world, the Liberian Civil War officially began. Unofficially the war had begun ten years earlier. It all started with rice.

Liberians don't just like rice—they love rice. It's their favorite and by far their most important food. President William Tolbert wanted Liberians to grow their own rather than relying on the heavily subsidized imported rice. He reasoned that if people stayed in the interior and planted rice, there would be less competition for the relatively few jobs in the cities. To encourage people to plant this most important crop, Tolbert was considering decreasing the government subsidy on imports by four dollars per hundred-pound bag. The new plan would drive up the price of rice around the country.

People panicked, fearing they wouldn't be able to afford rice at the increased price. Critics noted Tolbert stood to gain handsomely—he owned a huge rice farm. On April 14, 1979, two thousand activists took to the streets for a peaceful march on the presidential mansion. Later, when thousands of troublemakers joined them, the peaceful demonstration became an uncontrolled mob. Police confronted the demonstrators, hoping to keep things from getting even more out of hand. Someone fired a weapon. Instantly mayhem broke out and an orgy of looting lasting twelve hours tore up the city. Tolbert's military did not stop it. In fact, they led it.

By the time peace was restored at least forty people were dead and more than five hundred injured. The city, awash in guilt, waited for reprisals. There were multiple arrests and due process was suspended for those the President considered guilty of the original demonstration. People wondered what terrible fate awaited the oh-so-guilty military.

None. President Tolbert did absolutely nothing to punish the errant soldiers. They learned quite a valuable lesson. The President would not—or could not—stop them from doing whatever they pleased.

Less than a year after the fateful Rice Riot seventeen enlisted men of the Armed Forces of Liberia, including Master Sergeant Samuel Doe, shot and then disemboweled President Tolbert. This ended what had been an almost unbelievably long era of stable, although admittedly corrupt, years of governance. A few days later, after mock trials, thirteen high-ranking government ministers, some members of Tolbert's immediate family, were convicted of treason, tied to poles erected on Monrovia's Atlantic beach and shot to death.

The killers were proud of their work. Bodies, including the President's, were thrown into a common grave. High-ranking government ministers passed over for the ocean-side killings were tried (without benefit of lawyers), found guilty and executed. During the months of bloody retribution following Tolbert's assassination, Americo-Liberians fled in droves, many to the United States. Ironically, more than 150 years after freed slaves left U.S. shores, their descendants returned.

The natural order of things had flipped overnight. Since its founding in 1847, descendants of former U.S. slaves had governed Liberia. Now Master Sergeant Samuel Doe of the Krahn ethnic tribe was head of State. Many favored this new turn of events, assuming the vast majority of the population who were not Americo-Liberians would now be more fairly represented. Besides, there was little will to fight him. Memories of bodies tied to poles on the beach spoke loudly to the futility of resistance.

It would seem it's easier to kill a president than to be a good president yourself and soon there was trouble in Doe's self-made paradise. Doe was a military man, not a politician. He was woefully unqualified educationally and stumbled through the presidential speeches that had obviously been written by others. In 1983 his vice president, Thomas Quiwonkpa of the Gio tribe, fled the country after being accused by President Doe of attempting to overthrow the government. Doe became increasingly paranoid and insulated himself with members of his Krahn ethnic group.

In 1985, after five years of being Liberia's military dictator and under a cloud of controversy, Doe declared himself victor of Liberia's long-awaited presidential election. While at first reluctant, the United States eventually accepted the results, giving him the credibility he needed on the world stage. His massive ego empowered, he wished to be called "His Excellency the President Doctor Doe." His birthday became a national holiday and "Doe dollars" the currency.

Not surprisingly, many weren't as thrilled by his victory as was the newly-elected president himself. In fact, soon after the 1985 election Thomas Quiwonkpa was back. He staged an assassination he was sure would do the job. And unlike the first attempt, this time there was absolutely no doubt about his guilt. It was a choreographed event and when word went out over national radio, as per schedule, that President Doe was dead, people in Monrovia danced in the streets.

The announcement, however, was premature. The very much alive and humiliated President Doe was not dancing. He was absolutely furious. The chopped-up body parts of the former vice president were paraded through Monrovia's streets. Quiwonkpa's accomplices were put on trial and many summarily executed.

President Doe's hatred for his archenemy Thomas Quiwonkpa now extended to Quiwonkpa's entire tribal family, the Gio. In retribution for the attempted assassination people were killed simply for being Gio. Tribal rivalries around the entire country roused from their semi-slumbering state.

Chapter 4: An Uncivil War

The 1985 election and subsequent attempted coup of President Doe took place just months before we went to Liberia for the first time. While it was a concern and we recognized it wasn't as stable as it had been in the past, the bottom line was that Liberia was still open to the gospel. We had no way of knowing that a relatively unknown Liberian was at that time formulating a plot that would change the course of our lives, and the lives of countless others, forever. His name was Charles Taylor and he was a street-smart, smooth-talking Americo-Liberian man with a massive grudge.

A former employee in the Doe government, Taylor, like Doe himself, had taken full advantage of his position. When the president charged him with embezzling $922,000 of government funds, Taylor fled to the U.S. where he'd previously been educated. President Doe, now in good standing with the U.S., asked the American government for Taylor's arrest and got it.

Detained in an American prison in Massachusetts with nothing but time on his hands to think and plot, Taylor became a formidable foe indeed. After sawing through a window bar in an unused laundry room, Taylor and four fellow inmates escaped using knotted sheets. He traveled to Libya where he was met by a small band of Liberians with a shared mission—the ousting of President Samuel K. Doe. During our first wonderful term in Liberia we, and almost all of Liberia, were blissfully unaware that Taylor and his men were preparing for war at a terrorist training camp.

On Christmas Eve 1989 as we ate turkey in Wisconsin, Taylor and his estimated 100 plus cohorts crossed from the Ivory Coast and attacked the government soldiers stationed in the small town of Butuo in Nimba County. To someone ignorant of Liberian politics and geography the choice of this town as an entry point could seem insignificant. Contrarily, Taylor's plan was both brilliant and diabolical.

Nimba County was home to those of the Gio and Mano tribes, and President Doe handled the insurgency with the complete political incompetence Taylor no doubt knew he would. When President Doe sent his largely Krahn army to put out a relatively small Gio fire, his soldiers decimated entire villages for offences as small as giving food to Taylor's soldiers.

Angry government soldiers entered towns and villages shooting to kill. Husbands and wives were separated as they ran in opposite directions. Children unable to keep up were lost in the chaos. Doe's soldiers threw hundreds of babies into water-filled wells. Everyone wanted to be somewhere else. Anywhere else. Despite the unimaginable hardships and uncertainties of travel, mainly on foot, people fled by the thousands to neighboring Guinea or the Ivory Coast.

Needless to say, the government soldiers made themselves and the entire Doe government they represented a stench in the nostrils of the Gio and Mano tribal people. Seeking revenge for atrocities against their families, many joined Taylor's rebel force, the National Patriot Front Liberia (NPFL). Calling themselves "freedom fighters," their ranks swelled first by hundreds and then by thousands. The new recruits were untrained and, besides the obvious motive of revenge, joined for a wide variety of additional reasons as well. Whatever control Taylor had of his NPFL was soon lost.

In the United States, news reports on the British Broadcasting Company's *Focus on Africa* were our lifeline. Desperate to find out what was happening in Liberia, we tuned in to the BBC three times a day on a borrowed short-wave radio. While aware of the original coup of 1980 that resulted in the death of President Tolbert and the two attempted coups of President Doe since then, we had, nevertheless, projected America's peace on Liberia. We simply couldn't imagine any of what was happening now could lead to a long, drawn-out conflict.

Mark called our missionary friends in Monrovia often. They were in touch with our Tappita coworkers through short-wave radio two times a day. They assured us our coworkers were fine. Like us, they were hoping and praying the unrest would end soon. They planned to sit it out. After all, it was unthinkable that after more than fifty consecutive years in a relatively peaceful Liberia, Baptist Mid-Missions' missionaries would be forced to leave.

However, in March of 1990 the American embassy sent a message via radio to our coworkers that shattered all hope. Unbelievably, World Evangelistic Crusade missionaries Tom and June Jackson, who lived just thirty miles from our Tappita home, had been caught in the crossfire between invading rebels and the locally-stationed government soldiers who tried to use them as human shields. They were dead.

The embassy ordered all Americans to evacuate immediately. It was clearly unsafe to stay any longer. Taking only what was necessary our missionary friends piled themselves, their children and their most vulnerable Liberian friends into the mission airplane and the few vehicles available and headed for Monrovia.

Radio Station Building in Tappita

Within minutes of the last missionaries' departure, rebel soldiers took over our Tappita mission compound. They'd been waiting in the bushes. And these weren't just any rebels. Unbelievably, the mission property had been chosen by Charles Taylor himself to be his new NPFL headquarters. Our house was now a barracks for his freedom fighters and the radio station Mark worked tirelessly to build, the first broadcast bringing tears of joy to our eyes, was now "Radio 1," the voice of the National Patriotic Front of Liberia.

The Bible school students and their families were caught completely off-guard by the suddenness of the take-over by the NPFL. They rushed off the mission in all directions, literally running for their lives. These people near whom we'd lived, with whom we'd shared meals and laughed, were swept up in the tragedy and we were absolutely powerless to help them. The war was no longer faceless to us.

Some rushed toward the country's borders, trying to get out of Liberia. Others joined the thousands upon thousands heading to Monrovia, many of whom were on foot, with loads on their heads and children on their backs. The elderly and the infirmed—the lucky ones—were pushed in wheelbarrows. Others too weak to flee were left behind to face whatever happened unprotected and undefended.

Hundreds of checkpoints, both government and rebel, sprang up. To their horror people found human entrails roped across roads forming makeshift gates. Heads atop poles on either side stared sightlessly at the gathered crowds. Getting through the gates was a horrible ordeal. Anything and everything was an excuse to kill. People were killed for not standing still enough in line, for being a member of the "wrong" tribe—which, of course, varied from checkpoint to checkpoint—or if at a soldier's command they refused to kill their own relatives. People were told their lives had less value than chickens' lives and no one doubted the crazed soldiers meant it. Once in Monrovia, after days of travel, the displaced sought refuge with friends and relatives. The overflow found shelter in schools and churches. People were hungry, cold and bone weary.

Each day Taylor's forces were gaining more ground. As they drew closer and closer to Monrovia, fear gripped the city. Everyone knew when Taylor's rebel forces confronted Doe's government soldiers it would be very bloody.

On July 29, 1990, President Doe and a large group of government soldiers walked Monrovia's gorgeous Atlantic beach to Saint Peter's Lutheran Church where hundreds of displaced Mano and Gio Liberians prepared for sleep. In an exercise of unimaginable cruelty, the soldiers opened fire. They killed and killed and killed, some with bullets and many more with machetes, until the last scream was silenced. Over six hundred Liberian people were slaughtered as their President watched.

This horrific act precipitated the inevitable clash. And the chaos was actually much worse than people had originally feared. Taylor's forces had fractured when Prince Johnson, a subordinate with a lot of military experience and clout, coveted the many opportunities afforded by command and left, taking many men with him. So now instead of fighting the government soldiers, Taylor's NPFL were fighting them and rival rebel factions as well. Murder was without consequence and rape became a weapon of war.

The rebel soldiers were undisciplined and looting went completely unchecked. In fact, they considered the spoils of war their pay for fighting. Without a thought for the future of their country, multimillion-dollar pieces of equipment were sold for scrap metal, electrical wires were ripped off poles and stores representing entire life-savings stripped. "Steal from steal make God laugh," people snickered as one general stole from another only to have his loot taken by a third.

The local sports stadium teemed with people seeking safety and shelter. Others crouched in their homes as bullets rained down. An unattended wound often meant death. A mother's death meant death to her nursing baby. Thousands were killed and many more wounded as the fighting went on and on. Lest their concern for a burial draw negative attention, people were afraid to pick up their dead. Decomposing bodies littered the streets.

Food was in desperate shortage. Zoo animals and pets were eaten. Everything remotely edible was consumed. Taylor's army seized the Mount Coffee Dam hydroelectric facility, stopping city electricity and, even more devastating, the water supply. Illiterate people, wracked with thirst, opened cans of insect spray and ingested death.

Originally people from the interior had assumed if they were in Monrovia they'd be safe. Now everyone desperately wanted to leave, but only a lucky few could. The foreigners. They made their way to the U.S. embassy where on August 6, 1990, 225 United States marines with helicopters ferried them from the compound to the Marine vessel awaiting them off the Atlantic coast.

Shortly after, on August 17, Baptist Mid-Missions' Monrovia headquarters was raided and looted. An American man who had stayed, hoping to protect a group of Liberian friends, was shot. The soldiers took him, wounded and bleeding, to their headquarters. His dead body was turned over to the United States embassy a few days later.

Baptist Mid-Missions' Monrovia property after devastation by looters

Two and a half months after the massacre in St. Peter's Lutheran Church the bodies were still there, maggots crawling over rotting and decomposing flesh. President Doe could not stop the groundswell of hatred against him and his military. "The best Doe is a dead Doe," Taylor reportedly declared.

Soldiers sent by the Economic Community of West African States (ECOWAS) arrived in Liberia. This multinational force of three thousand soldiers was assigned the formidable task of holding back Taylor's progress. However, the ECOWAS peacekeepers were unable to stop the September 9, 1990, capture of President Samuel Doe. Rebel leader Prince Johnson's soldiers proudly videotaped an ear being cut off the shirtless, sweating and crying President. Johnson, who obviously saw no problem with his men being videotaped torturing Doe, alternated between strumming on a no-doubt looted guitar, sipping a Budweiser and screaming at the tortured President, "Where's the money!"

When we heard the news of President Doe's death, gruesome though it was, we were relieved. From the beginning Taylor had claimed that his goal was to rid the country of President Doe so new, democratic elections could be held. We desperately wanted to believe him and so thought that surely now, with Doe dead, the war would be over. We were sure that within weeks we'd be able to return to our home in Tappita. I imagined some babies or small children orphaned by war would need my help. I was full of plans for my future, which I hoped would look an awfully lot like my past.

Chapter 5: Refugees

Taylor lied. The war was not over. In fact, the looting, fighting and killing continued unabated.

To make matters even more complicated, the capture and death of President Doe lifted rebel leader Prince Johnson in his own eyes and the eyes of the people. Since Doe had become president by killing Tolbert, Prince Johnson felt that the capture and subsequent death of President Doe should give him the presidency. There was a certain twisted logic to it.

While for the life of me I couldn't figure out why *anyone* would want the position, Liberia now had four men claiming to be president: former President Doe's Vice President Harry Moniba, rebel leader Prince Johnson, rebel leader Charles Taylor and, last but not least, the man who was backed by the West African troops and thus controlled Monrovia, Amos Sawyer. It was a naked struggle for power.

Meanwhile, back in the United States, time was passing and churches were anxious for missionaries they supported financially to make decisions regarding their futures. Unable to return to Liberia, some resigned from the mission. Others chose to transfer within Baptist Mid-Missions to different countries and ministries.

For those who wished to continue working with Liberians, the options were limited. This was especially true for us. Our mission leaders had mandated that no missionaries with children still in the home could work anywhere inside Liberia. If we wished to continue to work with Liberians, the only choice we had was to work with those who were displaced by the war and living in neighboring West African countries.

After a brief survey trip to the Ivory Coast by two Baptist Mid-Missions missionaries, Mark and I decided together we would go there. True, we knew practically nothing about the Ivory Coast. True, no one we knew had ever worked among war refugees. But also true, we wanted to return to Liberia quickly when the war ended and being near the border was the surest way to make that happen.

Admittedly, the thought of "refugee work" was intimidating. But how different could it be from what we'd already done? After all, a Liberian is a Liberian. Besides, the war, as bloody as it was, couldn't last long—surely no more than six months. Surely. Then we could move back into Liberia and resume work with the radio station and the other ministries we loved. This refugee stint in the Ivory Coast would be very temporary.

Leaving for the Ivory Coast

In June of 1991 we left Minneapolis. Our children, ages four, six and eight, staggered under the weight of their fully-loaded carry-ons as we traveled from Minneapolis to Amsterdam to Sierra Leone to Abidjan. With us were our missionary friends Jeff and Kim Abernethy and their three daughters, the youngest a baby.

As we stepped out of the airplane and onto the tarmac of the Ivory Coast's Houphouët-Boigny International Airport, the humid night air hit us like a wave. Men in uniforms shouted at us in French as we entered the smoke-filled terminal. I mentally scrambled for anything from my one semester of eighth-grade French. I found only, "Would you like to see my apartment?" It was of no help. My mind froze and my heart raced with fear.

Having brought with us what our two families would need for the indefinite time that we expected to be in the Ivory Coast, between us we had thirty pieces of luggage. The chances of leaving the airport with all of it seemed mighty slim. God mercifully sent help. An American with another mission agency came to our rescue. But even so, it took a long time and a lot of fast, hard, unintelligible talking to get us out of the airport. A misunderstanding about our destination resulted in an unexpected tour of the city. By the time we settled in for the night at the missionary guesthouse, I was totally exhausted, overheated and overwhelmed.

The next day missionary nurse Ardith Maile joined us, completing our small team. As we were out and about we all noticed that tension hung in the air of Abidjan every bit as heavily as the tropical heat. Armed soldiers, for reasons we couldn't figure out, stopped cars asking for identification. They showed a distinct preference for vehicles filled with white faces. University students were rioting. At night we could hear the sound of exploding tear gas grenades from our guest rooms.

President Houphouët-Boigny was very old and perhaps even dying. Affectionately called Papa Houphouët, the beloved leader had mastered the political art of keeping everyone relatively happy while at the same time greatly enriching himself. He led the Ivory Coast to independence from France in 1960 and had held the office of President, basically uncontested, for the more than thirty years since then. Although the media did their best to downplay it, he was obviously in extremely precarious health. Everyone wondered who would take his place when he died.

Needless to say, the city did not feel hospitable and after two weeks in Abidjan we were more than ready to leave. We knew little about Péhe (pronounced "Pay"), our intended destination, except that years ago Baptist Mid-Missions' missionaries had built two houses and a small guesthouse on a piece of property near the edge of the village and that it had been a while since any missionary had lived in them.

So with all of our belongings packed into and on top of a small, rickety "bus" and covered by a tarp, our missionary team headed for that unknown location several hundred miles down the road. There was barely room to sit, but we didn't care. We were just glad to be leaving Abidjan. Things would be easier in Péhe. They simply *had* to be.

Not necessarily true. After endless travel in the driving rain and sitting at military checkpoints for hours on end, we arrived at four o'clock in the morning at what felt like the very edge of the earth. And it became painfully obvious almost immediately that we were not in prewar Liberia and this certainly was not our beloved Tappita.

Our first full night in Péhe as we prepared our three small children for sleep, I looked up and was surprised to see a young teen girl standing amid our opened Action Packers. Without preamble she announced that her mother had sent her to ask us for bluffing powder. Bluffing powder? While I may not have understood what in the world she was asking for, I clearly understood it was inappropriate for a total stranger to let herself in unannounced. To my dismay, I also saw the young girl didn't share this understanding with me.

When refugees had fled from Liberia to the Ivory Coast, every town and village anywhere near the border was flooded with people desperate for shelter. Seeing their need, Péhe's church leadership allowed Liberians to build houses along the edge of the mission property. By the time we arrived in 1991 several hundred Liberian war refugees lived in Péhe, many in a long row of mud-stick houses parallel to the mission's cement-block structures. Most were without jobs, farms and schools. Time hung heavy on their hands.

And unfortunately we, their new white-skinned neighbors, were endlessly fascinating. The noise, confusion and crowds appeared limitless as children, both Liberian and Ivorian, ran among the cows, goats, chickens and guinea fowl that inhabited our yard. They chased the five missionary children around, pushing at them playfully. But the missionary children, overwhelmed with the sheer number and the unfamiliar languages, shrank back and moved between their houses in a tight pack, fortifying themselves against the inevitable onslaught. Without shame the African children crowded against the screened door and pressed their faces into the windows to watch us eat.

Meanwhile Liberian and Ivorian men alike took advantage of the newly cut field alongside our houses by playing endless games of soccer. Practice began at the crack of dawn, although the regular games weren't played until later—men on the field and children between the missionaries' houses. Women sat on the tiny porch in front of our guesthouse and cheered for the men at the top of their lungs. Sometimes the crowds neared two hundred people. Privacy became a luxury no money could buy.

Everyone wanted to be my friend. People from Péhe as well as the surrounding villages and towns came to visit. We were rich Americans and obviously we'd come to give them things. Their job was clarifying what they needed and wanted most—our job was supplying it. Some verbal and some written, we received thousands of requests for everything from rain boots to full-ride scholarships to colleges in the U.S. While we did have some funds for relief projects, Baptist Mid-Missions was not a refugee agency. We were in no way equipped to deal with the needs of these thousands upon thousands of people, but no one knew that. Their expectations were huge and their visits regular.

And I was a "pleaser"; I wanted everyone to be satisfied with me. But no matter what I did, it was never, never, ever enough. If I ever did satisfy someone that very fact made it all the more likely the person would be back to ask for more. Every day, more and more requests. More and more hopes placed squarely in my lap by the refugees. And, of course, my husband and children had expectations as well. I worried about all the expectations. I worried about the war. I worried about the children. Most of all I worried about me.

In a fit of enthusiasm I started a hand-sewing class and gave out free cloth for projects. This ballooned to horrific proportions with ever-skyrocketing expectations. When I heard that mud-stick "hotels" were being built to house the influx of people moving to Péhe to get a few yards of free cloth, I cringed. With great embarrassment I realized that my project, which had seemed like such a great idea when I thought of it, had turned into a nightmare that was affecting our entire missionary team. My whole life was spinning madly out of control and I was completely and utterly spent.

Already seriously stressed, few emotional reserves remained for the nightmare that followed. While the refugees living in Péhe called themselves our friends, they proved themselves otherwise when two Gio men traveled from inside Liberia to welcome us back to Africa. An elderly man claimed these two visitors had personally slaughtered his family during the assault on their Krahn village. His adult daughter, a woman whom we'd helped on many occasions, took the story and ran with it. Although we knew it couldn't possibly be true—one was in the Tappita Bible School at the time the village was taken—the excitement intoxicated the crowd and truth became irrelevant. We brought the visitors into Abernethy's house for protection and before we realized what was happening, a full-fledged riot was on our hands. Hundreds of people gathered in the yard—some friend, some foe. Enraged young men screamed obscenities at our guests through the screened windows.

"We don't want you—we want them," the spokeswoman told me. "Just send them out and we'll leave you alone."

Screaming and cursing, wild-eyed young men rocked the car the three times Mark attempted to drive the visitors to safety in the ancient Russian Lada we'd borrowed. Three times he was stopped. The darkness of night made the situation even more frightening. These people wanted violence and, unbelievably, we'd become their enemies by thwarting them. Bloodlust lit the eyes in the windows.

Several Ivorian church leaders joined us, trying to figure out what to do next. The mayor from a nearby town came after hearing of the trouble and suggested his bodyguard use his gun to scare the crowd away. The nightmarish situation posed no obvious solutions. We prayed for God's wisdom and protection, both so desperately needed.

Finally an Ivorian friend slipped out of the house and was able to hail a motorcyclist for a ride to the nearest town. Close to midnight the military police roared into the village, sirens blaring. The crowd dispersed as a vapor. By the time the officers left, taking our visitors with them, it was well past midnight. The riot had lasted seven impossibly long hours. Still stunned by the complete incredulity of the entire event, we crawled into bed to sleep fitfully for the remainder of the short night. In the distance a lone drum beat.

My heart practically jumped out of my chest when early the next morning a line of men ran directly by the window of our tiny bedroom, "*Un, deux, trois, quatre*," they chanted loudly and in unison. My mind raced. Had the beating drum I heard in the night been a call to arms? Were these men coming to kill us?

No, they were soccer players counting in unison as they ran to the field for yet another predawn exercise session. This ended any chance of sleep. As became my habit, I curled up in the bed, drew the sheet over my head and wished myself someplace else. Anyplace else. With no reliable car, phone, ham radio or local post office, I felt entirely isolated and totally trapped. I hated my life.

In the days following Black Monday, as we came to call it, the worst offenders came offering excuses and weak, halfhearted apologies. Requests for financial or material assistance often followed these "apologies." It galled me. How could they do this to us? Asking us to help them by day and willing to kill us by night?

Although the immediate threat passed, the environment making Black Monday possible remained. Innocent babes that we were, it took something as big as a riot for us to figure out that the Liberians didn't consider us above taking sides—perhaps even participating—in their war. We were "Gio lovers" who had lived for more than three years in Nimba County. Now we were living in an almost 100 percent Krahn area. These were the two primary warring tribal groups. While we were not living inside Liberia, we nevertheless lived with the tensions Liberia's war created.

Sickness haunted us. The children all got chickenpox. Then John-Mark and Nathan came down with horrible cases of malaria that normal treatment didn't cure. Both boys' fevers soared to 105 degrees and we had no ice to cool them. Ardith cried as she gave them injections of quinine. "What have I done, bringing my family to this place?" my normally unflappable husband moaned.

I missed the chicken pox and malaria. Instead I got dysentery. It shouldn't have been a surprise considering it was rainy season and we lived downhill from people who didn't believe in outhouses. ("Why would you want to pack it all in one place?") Additionally, we shared our yard with any number of livestock who manufactured manure that an interesting variety of exotic species of flies seemed more than a little attracted to.

Besides the disease symptoms themselves, I suffered all fifteen possible side effects of the medication. I was so weak I could barely walk. Loud noises reverberated in my head, making me feel crazy. My pathetically skinny body seemed an appropriate home for my flat, lifeless eyes. I went from depressed to suicidal.

After three months in Péhe, just when I thought I couldn't stand another day, a duplex opened up in Toulépleu, a nearby town of several thousand people. Our entire team could now leave. With only one small vehicle to transport goods and people, several trips were necessary. When we completed the move, with immense relief I said to Mark, "We are finally alone!" That was a telling declaration considering the Abernethy family, Ardith and a Liberian couple were also in the apartment with us for the night.

Our missionary team was totally exhausted. The day after we moved from Péhe to Toulépleu we left for Abidjan to get some rest and pick up desperately needed supplies. Mark, John-Mark, Nathan and Ardith rode a commercial bus while the Abernethys, Melodie and I squeezed into the small Lada. I announced by way of encouragement as we took off, "It can't get worse."

Wrong. It can *always* get worse. At multiple checkpoints manned by unsmiling military police carrying AK-47s and pistols, we were stopped for inspection. "Who are you? Where are you going? Show us your documents!" they demanded gruffly in French.

And then there were the problems with the Lada. The final breakdown, the one no tinkering could fix, was at four in the morning—directly in front of a village. I cringed when, with dawn's first light, the villagers awoke and dozens of strangers gathered to stare at us. Kim Abernethy, the only one of us who knew enough French to communicate, was sent to Abidjan with a carload of strangers to find help. Eventually we were rescued. Hours later at a guesthouse in Abidjan, exhausted and filthy, I threw my head down on the table and sobbed, "I feel like someone is chasing me with fire!"

Several other missionary families joined our ministry team. While this helped with the workload, it also brought brand-new tensions to my already stressful life. After Taylor and his men left the mission property and relocated their headquarters elsewhere, some of the students had returned. In an attempt to keep the Bible school open the missionary men decided to make regular, weeklong teaching trips into Liberia, two men at a time. Mark took his scheduled turns and each time I kissed him good-bye, I wondered if I'd ever see him again.

As in Péhe, people came to our house constantly. The sheer volume of demands on our time, resources and emotional energy was staggering. We couldn't possibly do all we were asked to do. I hated the visits that included complaints we weren't doing enough and that what we were doing was being done poorly or for the wrong people. I hated the requests riddled with obvious lies. Most of all I hated all the expectations. If no one was presently at the door asking for something, I panicked thinking about those who were no doubt on their way.

A toxic mixture of fear, resentment, self-pity and depression haunted me. I was saying I loved the Liberian people—I was a missionary, after all—yet deep down I hated them. Not each individual, of course, but I absolutely hated the pressure I felt to satisfy a group of people with insatiable needs. I thought of missionaries scattered throughout the world *not* suffering for Christ. I was jealous of them all. I thought of my twin sister living her simple, idyllic life in rural Tennessee. How could both of us be in God's will? It wasn't fair!

By this time suicidal thoughts were habitual. In the darkness of night while waiting to fall asleep, I thought of death. It was my secret and delicious preoccupation. I desperately wanted my life over. The war just seemed to go on and on, and the thought of years of living among these people brought on despairing thoughts I had no will to fight.

Mark didn't understand why I was floundering. When I voiced my many concerns to him, his standard response was a slightly annoyed, "Don't worry about it." Don't worry about it? *How?*

I felt tremendous pressure from him to succeed—whatever *that* meant. "Buck up!" seemed Mark's unspoken command. Knowing he was committed to these people while I was inwardly counting the years until we could retire or secretly thinking of ways to kill myself left me feeling hopeless, embarrassed and guilty.

"Have you been having your devotions?" Ardith asked after I dumped on her one day. If only it were so simple! Yes, I was having my devotions! But I obviously didn't know this God to whom I prayed and whose Book I read. I couldn't believe a God of love had taken my offer of missionary service—to *Africa,* no less—and turned it on me this way.

Refugees

Our mission home-office personnel encouraged us to take breaks—go somewhere for a vacation. However, we were new in a strange, French-speaking country and didn't even know where we could go. I begged Mark to let us go back to the U.S. for a break, but because of the expense he felt it was out of the question. Our "vacation getaways" were tense, bustling supply trips to Abidjan.

On one such trip Mark and I took Ardith to Abidjan's airport. We left our children—ages five, seven and nine—in Toulépleu with missionary friends. After dropping Ardith off and settling into our guesthouse, Mark left to get supper. An hour later he returned, distressed. A policeman had stopped him and asked for identification. When he couldn't produce a visa, the officer confiscated his passport.

My heart froze in fear. If this were a scam, Mark's passport was gone and we couldn't travel. We could neither return to our children nor communicate with them the reason we did not return. With absolute abandonment of pride or pretense and beyond caring what other guests thought of me as my cries carried out the screened windows, I sobbed so hard I was practically howling. This moment in time seemed to encapsulate my entire life. We were trapped! Absolutely everything was out of control. My life was one big horror from which there was never, ever, even one moment of true escape.

Mark looked at me—my face twisted with anguish and soaked with tears—and then stated the obvious. "Maybe we do need a break."

The next day Mark got his passport back and as we returned to Toulépleu and our children, I felt hope for the first time in months. Because of a serious back problem that had been causing Mark a lot of pain and my desperate and ongoing "head problem" that had been causing both of us a lot of pain, Mark, to my great relief, had decided a trip back to the States would be money well spent.

A year after our arrival in the Ivory Coast we flew back to Minnesota to spend the summer with Mark's parents. Our coworkers flew back at the same time, separating from us in New York. I felt we'd escaped a war, which indeed we had.

Chapter 6: The Confrontation

Back in Minnesota our families and friends welcomed us warmly. However, glad though they were to see us, they were very concerned over how stressed-out we looked. Particularly me.

"You know God won't be mad at you if you don't go back," our pastor said by way of greeting. He was concerned lest a false sense of guilt motivate us to return. Our mission's leaders were also concerned; burned-out missionaries might quit mission work altogether. Mark's mother privately counseled Mark to consider my needs. What good would his mission work be if he lost his family? My mother, ever the encourager, was summarily silenced when, questioning my exclusively-negative spin on the year, I emotionally declared, "When I get to heaven God is going to have to explain to me the passage, 'My yoke is easy and my burden is light.' This burden is very, very, very heavy!"

Away from the refugees and basking in the beautiful summer sunshine, I eventually began to unwind. The haunted look left my eyes. It was beyond wonderful to have the amazing and most precious of all possible luxuries—privacy—once again available to me. I hoped the summer would never end. I *willed* it to never end.

With strength renewed and emboldened by the many people who felt God couldn't *really* expect me to go back to refugee work, I decided we should move on. The only thing standing between a better life and me was Mark.

I assailed Mark with reasons we should quit. Our missionary coworkers, rather than returning with us as planned, were transferring to another country. The war was increasing in intensity and there was no end in sight. Our commitment was to Liberia, not the Ivory Coast. The Ivory Coast was unsafe; could he not remember Black Monday? Besides, I didn't like it there one little bit. On and on I went—Mark and I in a verbal battle of the wills. I was quite unashamedly the other Proverbs woman. The "drippy-faucet" one. Obviously Mark was a hard nut to crack so he needed more than average persistence.

Public opinion was in my favor. Everyone on the west side of the Atlantic was either neutral or agreed with me. Mark was the only person in my present world who actively believed the Ivory Coast and its ministry to refugees was the right choice for us.

While I more publicly bargained with Mark, privately I bargained with God. I would go anywhere, do anything—just let it be someplace else. Since God obviously wanted me to be suffering and I hated cold weather, I negotiated with God about Siberia or Alaska. I didn't care if I never saw the sun again, I just didn't want to go back to those people!

After several weeks of active campaigning, Mark approached me one afternoon and announced we needed to talk. Sitting beside me on the edge of the bed, in his logical manner Mark told me what he thought of my attitude about going back to the Ivory Coast. In a word, unimpressed. In fact, he told me in no uncertain terms that he was very disappointed in me. In the past we'd worked together as a team, but now he felt like he was trying to drag me around the world against my will. He then outlined what he saw as our responsibility to the refugees, what he felt had already been accomplished, what remained to be accomplished and, lastly, his hopes for a future back in Liberia.

I sat quietly listening. What was the point of talking? There was no question that everything Mark said was true. While this ministry to refugees was terribly difficult, many had come to Christ through Bible studies, church services and evangelistic meetings. The harvest really was ripe. But I knew I was right too. Refugee work *was* horrid. The people *were* ungrateful. It *wasn't* what we'd signed up for. The war *did* change everything. Obviously we shouldn't go back!

Mark went on and on. Then, after his forty-five minute "sermon," he gave an "invitation." He announced, "If you feel you *can't* go back, we won't. But if you simply don't want to, we will. So which is it?"

Which is it? Here was my chance! Yet at the moment that should have spelled victory and freedom, I felt almost as though God were grabbing me by the ears and saying with His sternest father's voice, "Think, Nancy! Think!" The issue instantly became much more complex. In fact, it seemed my very life hung in the balance.

After a very long silence during which I contemplated what I would say—how I would respond to this very unexpected and extremely well-worded presentation of options—I answered with complete honesty. "I can go back, but *I don't want to!*"

Looking squarely at me, immense relief showing all over his face, Mark took a deep breath and said, "OK, then we're going back. And you're going to have a good attitude about it."

Gulp. Was that it? No more discussion? No more negotiation? Having admitted to Mark that I *could* go back, he appeared absolutely determined to do just that—and sooner rather than later. Mark talked for a few more minutes, making it clear what he expected from me. Cooperation. He wanted me to get behind him and help pull things together so we could leave the U.S. as soon as possible. After all, it was already past the time we'd set aside for this break.

As I sat on the edge of the bed listening to Mark, I realized I had a choice to make. I could follow Mark's leadership even though I thought it was a big mistake or I could put my foot down. If I did as Mark was asking and went back, I knew exactly what my life would be like. Horrible. On the other hand, I knew I could refuse to go back and everyone would understand. In fact, they would support me. After all, who could possibly fault me for not returning to a life for which they'd never have considered volunteering in the first place?

O.K. I'd do it! I'd follow Mark back to refugee work if that were what he wanted so much. But this was *his* decision, not mine. If it were awful (and I was sure it would be), it would be his fault. If they killed him (and I thought they just might), it would be his fault. If we failed (and I was sure we would), it would be his fault. It was out of my hands.

I left the bedroom determined to do my best. If Mark wanted to make a poor decision, that was up to him. He certainly didn't need me working against him. I knew what refugee work was like and I didn't have to be a rocket scientist to know this plan was doomed. Mark would realize soon enough that I was right and then we would quit this ridiculously impossible ministry and go to some place decent.

Officially absolved of all responsibility for this decision, to my surprise my spirits lifted immediately. As we finished our shopping and took care of the many last-minute details of international travel I cooperated completely and cheerfully. What was the point of doing otherwise?

In early December 1992 we returned to the Ivory Coast loaded down with Rubbermaid Action Packers filled with ministry supplies and Christmas gifts for family and friends. Although still less than thrilled about Mark's decision to return to the Ivory Coast, I had to admit I was very glad to be out of Minnesota's cold winter.

Very unexpectedly I discovered my mood matched the tropical weather—sunny and bright. As we were out and about in Abidjan visiting with friends, dropping off Christmas presents and running errands, I noticed I didn't feel overwhelmed or stressed as I had the entire first year.

Two days after our arrival, as I rested in the afternoon at the guesthouse, I puzzled over my unexpected emotions. Something was different this time. Very, very different. And something was happening. What was this feeling? And it was heightening. Why was I so... so what? I felt totally light and free. Even with jet lag I felt buoyant. The contrast between my depression before our break and my joyous freedom now absolutely amazed me.

I moved to where Mark rested, my mind racing to sort out these feelings. It was all so overwhelming. "What's happening to me?" I asked, awe in my voice and tears streaming down my face. "What's *wrong* with me? Why do I feel this way? I feel different. I feel... *happy!*"

Joy? Yes, in fact, *full* of joy. It was glorious!

Was God showing me something through this overwhelming flood of joy I was experiencing? Had this surrender to Mark's leadership released me from a bondage of which I was previously unaware? I didn't know. But the one thing I did know for sure was that I felt free. And rather than wishing I could die, I reveled in all of the hope for my future.

That day for the first time I began to understand, if only in a small way, the spiritual significance of my surrender. It had been not only about obeying Mark and following his leadership, but also and more importantly about obedience to God. My choice to trust God's written Word by putting myself under my husband's authority—even when I totally disagreed with him—had greatly honored God.

In the days and weeks following I did a lot of thinking and analyzing. By making the initial decision together with Mark to pursue work among the refugees, I'd unintentionally "co-led" our family. Therefore the disaster that had become our lives was as much my responsibility as Mark's. The distinction between making the decision together and following his leadership was perhaps subtle, but it was, nevertheless, the source of my inner conflict. This time it was different. Mark was making the decision and I was following his leadership. The burden of responsibility was entirely his and I was then freed to focus on the responsibilities that were actually mine.

To my embarrassment, I now understood that horrid first year in refugee work had revealed who I really was and that while it was true that numerous people had sinned against me, I couldn't blame them for my reactions. I, Nancy Sheppard, was not a good girl sent by God to rescue my goofy, prankster husband. I was, in fact, a mess.

And although he hadn't fallen apart like me, Mark was becoming increasingly aware of the responsibility he carried for the crisis. He had not protected me enough either emotionally or physically. He'd asked me to do things that more rightly should have been his responsibility. Additionally, his leadership had been extremely passive at times, tempting me to fill the vacuum this created. Now, this second time around, we both knew that if we were going to survive, much less thrive, things needed to change.

Unlike our first year, I was now aware of how desperately I wanted Mark to lead. How desperately I *needed* him to lead. More humbled than I'd ever been in my life, I was actually scared of myself. I made the decision that no matter how passively expressed, no matter how difficult to discern, I would try to figure out what Mark wanted and then follow that leadership. Not surprisingly, once Mark understood I was actively watching and waiting for him to lead, he began to lead more clearly. Additionally, he stopped using the old and ineffective "Buck up" motivational strategy. He was much more careful to think through whether a particular project or ministry should, in fact, even be my responsibility. If not, he either took care of it himself or delegated it to someone else.

Mark and I both faced the fact that although we'd been living physically in the Ivory Coast, emotionally we had been in Liberia. This had created constant inner turmoil. We decided to call the Ivory Coast "home" and do what we could to make it feel that way. So instead of assuming I'd survive one way or another, Mark put his energies into fixing what was fixable. We made the house more livable, planted a garden, and, silly as it may sound, hired someone to sit outside our door and talk with strangers who came to us with requests. If it qualified for consideration, we were told about it. If not, the request was denied and the individual graciously sent on his or her way. This not only redeemed hours of each day, it allowed us to better resist the ever-present temptation to sacrifice the important on the altar of the immediate.

I was extremely grateful for anything that made my life easier. In appreciation for the many efforts I could see that Mark was making, I found myself trying harder than ever to please him. Mark, increasingly grateful that I'd followed him back to this less-than-idyllic life, was trying harder than ever to please me. It became somewhat of a contest to see who could please the other more. Not surprisingly with both of us consciously working on it, we fell deeper in love than we'd ever been.

While these mental and physical changes made our home life far more manageable, the reality of our situation outside the home hadn't changed. The consequences of living so near a war zone had weekly, if not daily, ramifications on our lives. Recruiters for the factions were constantly in and out of the area, looking for volunteers and stirring up tensions. Taylor's soldiers lobbed a bomb from Liberia into the Ivory Coast, killing several people. Thousands of terrified refugees ran from their homes. The Ivorian police became sick and tired of dealing with all the problems created by the refugees and announced they'd kill anyone who in any way threatened them. When a refugee pulled out a knife in the market the police didn't arrest him—they shot him seven times.

Unfortunately for them, we were one of the problems with which the police and other local authorities constantly had to deal. We were forever being accused of involvement in the conflict. Those who thought the "missionary" explanation seemed unlikely came up with their own explanations for our presence at the edge of nowhere. Word on the street was that we were CIA agents working undercover for the U.S. government. The illogic of bringing children on this covert assignment didn't seem to faze the most ardent supporters of the position.

Once a missionary coworker was seen in his vehicle with a man who wore sunglasses like Charles Taylor's and was afterward accused of giving the big warlord himself a lift. The fact that Taylor was far too smart to hitchhike into the territory of his mortal enemies didn't seem to occur to them. To protect us from similar accusations in the future, local authorities forbade us to transport anyone whom we didn't know personally.

One day the Sous-Prefect, the man holding the highest government position locally, and several gendarmes startled me while I was sitting in the living room home-schooling my children. Without knocking they burst noisily into our duplex and demanded to know why there was a radio antenna in our yard. I yelped, "Mark!" and was astounded at the speed in which he appeared on the scene. As we hurriedly assured them we'd take it down, the gendarmes confiscated our missionary friend's ham-radio equipment for which the antenna was used.

Why the hubbub? We were being accused of being spies for Charles Taylor's rebels yet again. The evidence? While on the surface it appeared to be the radio antenna, by then we knew what the real "evidence" was. We had lived in Tappita for three years and therefore were obviously loyal to the Gio. Ironically, in Tappita we were accused of being loyal to the Krahn. The evidence? We hadn't reported a massacre plan. Surely we knew the Krahn were staging a massacre of the Gio since we lived among them.

In light of these and other such threats, I began to understand myself better. As scary as physical or political threats were, I had to admit I feared the expectations of people even more. I also had to admit that often my desire to please the Liberians was not so much that I wanted to help them as that I was afraid I'd disappoint them. I couldn't handle the look—the one that said, "I was counting on you and you've failed me." While sometimes I felt I'd actually failed the person or failed God, more often I was frustrated that I'd failed to communicate what a nice, kind, thoughtful and all-around-wonderful person I really was.

For the first time in my life I asked God to show me, really show me, how to release this awful burden of people-pleasing. He reminded me of Pilgrim from *The Pilgrim's Progress* putting his load down at the foot of the cross. I mentally began to do the same—put my load at the foot of the cross. When worry jumped back on me, I'd do it again. Over and over and over again. When I first started this procedure the load stayed down for only a couple of seconds or a minute. Eventually the burden stayed down for minutes in a row. With time I began enjoying a half hour, then an hour free of fear. As the weeks turned to months, I found myself almost entirely freed from the fears that had previously controlled my life.

"Nancy, you *have* changed," Ardith observed one day as I enthused about the Chinese dish I was putting together using local foods. She was certainly in a position to know since she was living with us. And there was no doubt that I had changed. Once again I was enjoying my family. Once again I was enjoying crafts and hobbies. I spent hours pouring over cookbooks, sewing clothes for my children and gardening.

We found a place in the Ivory Coast to go for breaks. San Pedro, a coastal city, had reasonably priced accommodations with the privacy we so desperately needed. As the children played, I stared at the ocean. The gigantic waves rolling in and then crashing madly against the huge rocks lent perspective to human troubles.

I thought of Jeremiah 5:22—"'Do you not fear Me?' says the LORD. 'Will you not tremble at My presence, Who have placed the sand as the bound of the sea, By a perpetual decree, that it cannot pass beyond it? And though its waves toss to and fro, Yet they cannot prevail; Though they roar, yet they cannot pass over it.'" God had set a boundary for the ocean. Something so massive was under His control. It gave me confidence that my life was also safe with Him.

As we neared the end of our second three-year term of service in 1994, the reality of the lessons God was teaching me was tested. Mark started feeling weird, painful sensations around his heart, especially when he was lying down. At first he wasn't unduly concerned, but after several weeks with the strange symptoms, he began to wonder if there was something seriously wrong with him. Finally, after a very bad couple of hours one day, Mark made a decision. We would go see a doctor in Ferké, a town in the north of the Ivory Coast, where there was a hospital staffed by English-speaking missionaries.

We quickly threw together some clothes and bathroom supplies and started on our way. As we left town I prayed aloud for safety as we traveled. Mark concentrated on his driving while the children played in the back seat. While concerned about his pain, I was thankful we were getting the help he needed and looked forward to visiting Ferké, a town I'd heard much about but never visited.

Disaster struck as we passed through Blolèquin, a moderate-sized town about an hour and a half drive from Toulépleu. It was a busy market day with hundreds of people milling around the grounds and spilling over into the road. Mark slowed the truck accordingly. We both noticed a young girl about twelve years of age who was paying no attention to the traffic as she chatted with a friend. Then we both saw her, without warning, turn from her companion and dash into the road directly in front of our vehicle. Mark slammed on the brakes as hard as he could and swerved the pick-up to miss her. Within seconds it stopped. However, it was too late. At the exact moment the truck stopped the girl was directly in front of it. She turned her head and looked me straight in the eye, complete surprise stamped on her face. The next instant she bounced off the hood with a sickening thud. "Oh, no!" Mark cried while the rest of us screamed with shock and horror.

The injured girl lay unconscious on the pavement. Although the only visible wound was a two-by-four-inch patch of peeling and slightly bloody skin on her leg, it was obvious by her eerie stillness that the situation was extremely serious.

There was nothing anyone was selling that was more interesting than what was happening on the road and within minutes hundreds of marketers had gathered to witness the spectacle. An accident like this was a nightmare for anyone anywhere, but in the Ivory Coast it was especially dangerous. We'd heard numerous stories of family members avenging the injured or dead by killing drivers. We were aware of our complete vulnerability to the crowd of people surrounding us.

While there was a hubbub of activity and commotion, no one was threatening in any way. And wonder of wonders, not one person implied the accident was Mark's fault despite the unconscious child lying on the pavement. The spectators were completely calm. Surprisingly, I too felt calm. I was able to comfort

The Confrontation

Mark at a time he desperately needed comfort and certainly *didn't* need a wife who was falling apart.

Several men appeared with a stretcher and whisked the girl to a local clinic. We drove to the gendarmerie where a crowd of people soon gathered. Several officers questioned Mark and me. It was tense, but again, we never felt threatened. Periodically someone came with a report from the clinic. Our hopes built when we were told there were no broken bones and the girl was doing better. Despite the encouraging reports after two hours the girl died, presumably from head injuries. Even then, upon hearing this news, I remained calm. I was able to reassure Mark who was crushed because he'd caused, however unwittingly, the death of a child.

Even as we sat in the strange office in a strange town, I analyzed my reaction to the tragedy. I was living in a nightmare, yet I felt calm and enveloped with the love and care of God. I was able to minister to Mark and my children rather than requiring comfort myself. I half expected to see the angels I sensed were surrounding us.

As we left the gendarmerie a series of questions ran through my mind. Most notably, why had God allowed this? I'd specifically prayed for safety as we left our home and yet this tragedy had occurred. But then, having allowed it, He ministered grace. For a person recently struggling with a serious fear problem, witnessing God's sustaining grace while a nightmare unfolded before my eyes was immensely reassuring.

We continued on to the mission hospital where Mark's medical problem was diagnosed. Thankfully rather than something really serious, Mark found it was a hiatal hernia—something that often mimicked the symptoms of heart trouble.

I found out some months after the accident that some on our missionary team secretly wondered if this event would be the proverbial "straw that broke the camel's back" and we'd quit our work among the Liberian refugees. When I heard this verbalized I realized how much I'd grown; the thought had not occurred to me. God was truly changing my fearful heart.

Chapter 7: Heidi

Returning to the U.S. for our second one-year home assignment in 1994, I was completely different from the haggard, self-focused woman of two years before. Joy was visible on my face. Something else was visible too. I was pregnant. On purpose.

John-Mark, Melodie and Nathan were eleven, nine and seven years old. Everyone assumed, like us, we were finished with the baby stage. However, as God worked in my heart about submission to Mark's leadership, He also revealed my faulty view of children—particularly *my* children.

John-Mark, Melodie and Nathan—1994

While I loved them dearly, I felt guilty for the time spent on my children's care. This thinking effectively nullified the importance of about ninety-five percent of my life. It wasn't that anyone was pressuring me to do something else with my time; I was pressuring myself. Guilt, guilt and more guilt.

It'd been worse when my children were younger and took

even more of my time and energy. Was anyone coming to Christ because of my wiping this toddler's nose? Did picking up these toys cause anyone to live more righteously? Was I even a good missionary if the bulk of my time was spent caring for my husband and children? Ironically, I knew taking care of other people's children had value—that was ministry. It was the value of caring for my own children that I questioned.

In my childhood and youth I was bombarded with an emphasis on full-time Christian service. As far as I was concerned, anything less than that was just a recipe for guilt. The truth was that while I could biblically refute any "saved by works" argument, I inadvertently practiced a "saved by grace, kept by works" theology. With guilt a driving force in my life, a flurry of Christian ministry made me feel safe. Surely it won me God's favor.

I read Mary Pride's book, *The Way Home: Beyond Feminism, Back to Reality*. The author challenged Christian women to consider if they were, in practice, really feminists. Had they inadvertently been sucked into modern, secular thinking?

I was so caught. While I had a degree in home economics from a Christian university and had taught all the right things at well-attended women's seminars, I knew that deep inside of myself I did not consider home my most important ministry. In fact, in the throes of parenting our three extremely active children I'd asked a friend to *slap* me if I ever talked about having another baby! Now, to Mark's delight and my chagrin, I knew God wanted me to have another child.

And so as we enjoyed our time in the U.S., I showed off my big belly. Surely people who saw Mark and me with our three elementary-aged children thought, "Oops!" But I knew better. This was most definitely a planned child. God's plan.

Heidi

Heidi and Melodie—1996

Heidi Suzanne Sheppard was born on September 27, 1994. As I held this tiny, perfectly formed baby I now understood that this was ministry. When I changed Heidi's diaper or wiped her runny nose, I was doing it first of all for God. When she was fussy and I calmed her, it was for God I did it. A loving kiss on her soft, little cheek was a kiss from God via my lips. I was nurturing a child whose soul would live on forever. I was a mother and my work was infinitely valuable in God's eyes.

Chapter 8: Surprised by the Power of Prayer

Liberia was making headlines around the world as the country with the truly horrific and bizarre war. The mind-numbing statistics—tens of thousands dead or displaced—were too overwhelming to comprehend. However, macabre news articles of fighters waltzing into battle wearing flowing gowns and women's wigs were truly unforgettable.

Drug-crazed fighters like General Butt Naked, who led his equally drug-crazed troops into battle wearing only lace-up boots, were infamous for their cruelty and complete disregard for human life. Pregnant women were  ripped open to determine the winner of a bet: boy or girl? Child sacrifice and cannibalism were commonplace.

World sympathy awoke to the plight of the large numbers of children, some as young as seven or eight, drawn into the conflict as soldiers. Their presence was common at the frontlines of battlefields, sometimes cradling rifles as tall as themselves. Children were desirable as soldiers because, once pumped with crack or any number of other available mind-altering drugs, they'd do what they were told without question.

When ECOWAS (the Economic Community of West African States) sent their "monitoring group," ECOMOG, to keep the peace, many of these 3000 soldiers, along with the others who later joined them, took sides in the conflict. Additionally, rather than helping the citizens, some found ways to enrich themselves at the citizens' expense. Looted goods were loaded into ships and disappeared. In the minds of Monrovia's increasingly cynical citizens, ECOMOG stood for "Every Car Or Moveable Object Gone."

Unable to take over Liberia's legitimate government, Taylor had created a parallel state of the massive amount of interior land he controlled. He called this area "Greater Liberia," and it was in constant conflict with Monrovia's various transitional governments. Throughout the remainder of Liberia there were multiple lower-level warlords fighting both Taylor and each other. Like Taylor, they coveted control of mineral mines, rubber, timber and anything else of possible value.

Since we were always hoping and praying for peace, it took several rounds of "peace accords" for me to figure out that the last thing a warlord wants is peace. The Liberians seemed to understand this better than us and were in no hurry to return. Tens of thousands remained in their mud-stick homes in Ivorian villages and towns. In June of 1995, traveling with four children through four international airports—Minneapolis, Zurich, Geneva, and finally Abidjan—we returned from our one-year home assignment in the United States to Africa and our work among the refugees.

After two weeks in Abidjan we journeyed to Bloléquin, where the fatal accident had occurred less than two years previously. Although because of the vivid memories it was the town where I least wanted to live, I knew it was where God wanted us to minister. Mark had been asked to construct and administrate a new mission clinic, as well as help with other ministries as needed. Our missionary team included three couples and Ardith Maile, my nurse friend who had lived with us in Touléupleu.

Our family was doing well. The children loved Africa and were cooperative with our mission work. They were also greatly enjoying their baby sister. Eight years younger than Nathan, the previous baby of the family, Heidi was growing up in a household of big people—and that worked for her. She was a princess

Surprised by the Power of Prayer

and we her public. It was obvious to us that Heidi was doomed to "spoilage" unless something radically changed. Competition was the obvious solution. I was pregnant again.

Rather unexpectedly since he was my fifth child, Jared's delivery was very long and painful. Our missionary team breathed a collective sigh of relief when nine pound, five-ounce Jared was born shortly after noon on March 18, 1996. I assumed the worst was over and looked forward to mothering my beautiful new baby boy.

Unfortunately, that wasn't the case. The worst was not over. Soon after his birth Jared began having very serious diarrhea. Because he was such a big baby, at first I was not unduly alarmed. However, as first days and then weeks passed with no change in his condition and Jared's abundant dimples and rolls disappeared completely, I realized something was terribly wrong. My mind raced with possible explanations—everything from a milk allergy to internal organ malformation.

I fought panic. I felt isolated from adequate medical help and from extended family and their support. What should I do? What *could* I do? Should Jared and I go to the States? While I'd never traveled internationally by myself—much less with a tiny baby—I was willing to do anything.

Jared, John-Mark, Melodie, Heidi and Nathan—1996

Finally, after weeks of concern, Ardith strongly suggested we have his stool checked for dysentery. She had said it before, but because it'd seemed so unlikely to be that—dysentery is most often contracted through contaminated food or water and Jared was a nursing baby—to my shame I hadn't followed through.

The lab test was positive. It was dysentery. We started Jared on the long course of treatment and despite my fear that he would respond to the medication as poorly as I had in Péhe, he suffered no apparent negative side effects. Within a week he started gaining back the weight he'd lost.

As Jared's health had been declining and he was getting skinnier by the day, Mark and I prayed like we never prayed for anything in our lives. We were far from the United States and its medical care and we felt desperate. We knew only God could help us. One day in the midst of our struggle, after another round of fervent prayers, Mark said, "Every term God has taught us something new. Maybe this term He's going to teach us how to really pray."

Now that was an interesting thought. Could God teach me how to really pray? I wanted it, but I seriously doubted it would happen.

Of course I prayed. I knew God had answered countless prayers. But prayer was incredibly hard work for me and in reality sometimes seemed like just another thing about which to feel guilty. I liked the old-fashioned quote, "Some pray. Some give. Some go." Obviously I was a "some go" person.

Soon after Jared's bout with dysentery, I was visiting our mission's clinic when a gray-haired man and woman brought in a three-month-old baby girl. The baby's unmarried mother had died soon after childbirth and there was no one to nurse her. After weeks of being fed only cornmeal and water, she weighed a mere six pounds and was nothing but skin pulled over bones. The baby was so weak and dehydrated the doctor was afraid her heart would stop beating while he listened with his stethoscope. It seemed obvious to me that what the grandparents were doing wasn't working and I asked if they'd considered placing the infant in an orphanage. They responded negatively and left, taking the frail child with them.

Normally the hopelessness of the situation would have frustrated me, but it didn't this time. I sensed this baby was a part of my life. I began praying for her regularly. Whenever I saw Dr. Burrows I asked about her. She had been brought back to the clinic several times for a variety of problems, he told me. Her weight and food situation remained unchanged.

Several weeks after that encounter at the clinic I heard someone outside our door. Looking down, I saw an elderly woman sitting on the step holding a tiny baby. I instantly knew who they were. The emaciated baby was clinging to life by the weakest of threads. Holding the child up to me, eyes soft with love and concern, the grandmother asked for help. The baby was dying and she knew it. I hurriedly made up several ounces of infant formula. Her grandmother and I watched with shared joy as the baby weakly sucked a few drops of the life-giving liquid into her bony frame. The elderly woman then handed me the baby and asked me to keep her.

With a mixture of relief and trepidation I accepted the little girl into our home. Obviously the last thing I needed was another baby—Jared was only three months old and Heidi twenty-one months. But God had prepared me. Since I saw the baby the first time, I'd known we were in some way connected. And now, with her in my home, at least I could stop worrying she'd die of starvation out in the village.

And so the baby, Felicia, became a part of our lives. Ever so gradually she began drinking more than a few drops of milk, and as she gained weight she also gained strength. A visiting American teenager was a tremendous help as she became Felicia's primary caregiver, allowing me to focus on Heidi and Jared.

Before I became overly concerned that I'd bitten off more than I could chew, an Ivorian friend came calling. "I want that baby," she announced.

"You want to help me care for her?" I questioned in my stumbling French.

"No, I want to keep her. I want her as my daughter." They'd lost a daughter through death, my friend told me. This baby girl would replace that child.

So it happened. Felicia became their daughter. And for several weeks everything went well. The baby was growing stronger each day and the family enjoying her immensely. The story seemed finished and the ending happy.

However, one day Felicia and her new mother were back. Pulling down the baby's diaper, my friend pointed to a weird, worm-like thing under her skin. Did I know what it was? she asked. I surely didn't. I suggested she take the baby to Dr. Burrows.

The doctor said it was a hernia. When Felicia cried really hard her tiny intestine came out of the hole in her abdominal wall. This happened regularly and each time it did, my friend took her to the doctor so he could push it back inside. Surgery would repair it, but Felicia was too young and far too weak to bear it.

Felicia's new mother and I were concerned. The baby was in serious pain when the intestine came out and it seemed awful to have to wait for several months for relief. We agreed the solution was to pray for God to heal her.

And so we did. Each day, sometimes many times a day, she and I prayed Felicia's hernia would be healed. There was no special gathering, no laying on of hands, no ceremony, no nothing. Just prayer. But as first days and then weeks passed without trips to Dr. Burrows, it became evident God had answered our prayers.

Now God really had my attention. I thought of the life-changing ramifications of our prayers for little Felicia and the potential this answer to prayer represented. For the first time in my life I understood I'd barely tapped into the amazing power that lay at my disposal. I began a very serious study of prayer. I was obsessed with books developing the subject and all biblical references to prayer. R.A. Torrey's *The Power of Prayer* and Norman Grubb's *Reese Howells: Intercessor* were tattered from multiple readings.

And rather than my somewhat haphazard methods of the past, I began praying in a determined and organized manner. I wanted God's power in my life more than anything. But even as I begged for His power, I knew I had it. It was the only possible explanation for my new and fervent desire to become a woman of prayer.

Chapter 9: The Emptying

During and immediately after Jared's bout with dysentery, a friendship I greatly cherished dissolved. This time it wasn't a Liberian, but rather an American, whom I couldn't satisfy. Attempts at reconciliation didn't produce a renewed closeness. The loss was searing.

The bile of fear rose in me. I began my all-too-familiar routine, trying desperately to satisfy her. It didn't do the job. The harder I tried the more impossible my situation appeared. I became acutely and painfully aware that, while I acknowledged it was impossible to please the Liberian refugees, it had never occurred to me I could be in the position where no matter what I did, it wouldn't satisfy a friend.

At the same time the loss of my friend isolated me socially, every ministry in which I was involved evaporated. Instead of being busy with missionary work, I had no missionary work to do at all.

The old Nancy would have panicked. Did the dissatisfaction and subsequent rejection of a friend mean God too was dissatisfied and would reject me? Would God love me as much in isolation as when active in obvious Christian service?

But now, rather than panicking, I recognized God was allowing this to happen so I could learn something very important. As awful as it was to be in this predicament, once and for all my question would be answered. Could the person of Jesus Christ replace the friendship and acceptance of people and the recognition accompanying Christian service? Could the invisible replace the visible? Bottom line: Was God enough?

I was in a very good position to test and see if I could be satisfied with His love alone. I was totally isolated from my family and friends in the States and although Mark was aware of what I was going through and cared deeply, I knew God didn't want me to suffocate him with details of the struggle with my friend.

If God was to become more important to me than "people friends," I needed to know Him. "Show me who You really are," I begged God. I was desperate to know from personal experience that He was who He said He was. I needed Him like I'd never needed anything before. I understood now what it meant to hunger and thirst for righteousness; I could almost feel it physically. I could live without food and water for a couple of days at least, but I didn't know if I could make it through the next minute without knowing God was holding on to me.

Not surprisingly, God pointed out to me that my fixation with satisfying Americans—my friend, Mark, others—was no more pleasing to Him than my fixation with satisfying Liberians. But how could I change? How could I stop caring what people thought of me? It was one thing to get over fixating on what Liberians thought of me, but to not care what my *friend* thought of me? What *Mark* thought of me? Being a "pleaser" was at the very core of my personality. Could I be changed that radically?

I poured out my desperate thoughts in prayer, and in answer to my prayer God opened my heart to continue His surgeon's work. It wasn't pretty. He revealed my pride. I was full of it.

Why did I think that despite my many faults, everyone should like me? Was that not pride? Why was I upset when my children misbehaved in public, but not nearly as upset about the same thing done privately? Was it not because their behavior made *me* look bad? When Mark was less than perfect, why was I so annoyed? Didn't I think I deserved only the best behavior and the best treatment from him? And of course the worst "sin" Mark could commit was to be unsatisfied with me—even if I was wrong!

As God revealed the various ways in which my pride manifested itself and I understood something to be sin, I confessed it and asked God for forgiveness. I begged Him for the strength to change. As I gained victory in one area God would reveal yet another manifestation of my pride. Yet because of His presence the

The Emptying

humiliation of having my many faults revealed was not only bearable, but something I actually craved. I felt His love surrounding me. In a way defying description I could feel Jesus walking with me through this intense struggle.

This wasn't just some theoretical experience; God made me put feet to it. A Liberian man to whom we'd been close became a real trial to our family and missionary team. While he still called himself a friend, his actions proved otherwise. Although resentment was in my heart, I felt I did an admirable job of keeping it almost invisible to the man himself. Additionally, because the possible ways my resentment showed seemed minuscule when compared to the hurt he regularly caused us, I felt justified. The Holy Spirit convicted me and made it clear I must apologize. Although I knew it probably would make no real difference in my relationship with this man, I understood clearly that any disobedience could damage my relationship with God. It was not a risk I was willing to take, so I asked forgiveness. This was just one of many relationship issues God asked me to make right.

One Sunday after a time of major acknowledgment and surrender of pride in yet another form, I arrived at church prayed up and 'fessed up. Surely today I was safe, I thought. While the sermon was interesting, it wasn't particularly convicting. There was nothing between God and me.

Jeff Abernethy, the missionary pastor, called for the invitation song, "I Surrender All." During the first verse the Holy Spirit nudged, *Go forward*. My heart pounded in stunned disbelief. Why was God doing this? He *knew* everything was confessed! Why was He asking me to do something so humiliating, especially since I was daily, consciously trying to keep a clean heart before Him?

Oh, help. There it was again. Pride. I wanted to root my feet to the spot and stay there until the miserable song finished, but I knew I couldn't do it. I had to obey. I'd found trying to satisfy others was hopeless and all I wanted now was God—and for Him to have me. Absolute submission was the only thing in my life that mattered. So I swallowed hard, stuck my foot determinedly into the aisle, and made my way to the front of the church. I felt God's smile for the act of obedience.

I found out pride has a twin sister—self-pity. At the time of Jared's first birthday, recalling the difficult labor followed by his sickness and then the rejection of my friend, I felt depressed. I was reliving the painful emotions and felt wrapped in a cloud of confusion. Why had God allowed this?

While on my knees pouring out these feelings to God, I felt Him ask me to thank Him for the very experiences I was resenting and resisting. Although I knew 1 Thessalonians 5:18 said, "In everything give thanks: for this is the will of God in Christ Jesus for you," I was, nevertheless, surprised by this thought. It seemed ridiculous to thank God for things so obviously negative. But since the command to give thanks for everything was solidly taught in scripture, I proceeded in prayer. At first it was stilted and felt insincere. After a couple of sentences, however, I found myself getting more into it. Eventually I really thanked God for the experience, my will leading my emotions.

When I finished thanking God, I felt Him ask me to compare it to Calvary. I realized, of course, that my pain and rejection were nothing when laid side-by-side next to His, yet I didn't feel that was the point God wanted me to understand. Instead I realized that because Jesus had lived as a man on earth and had experienced pain, He truly understood. He cared deeply about my pain and my hurts. God took away the load of unwanted emotions and left me feeling understood and cherished.

Each day, many times a day, I begged God to show me how to submit to the trial of my broken friendship. I desperately wanted to please Him, but I felt so scared and vulnerable. "'Perfect love casts out fear.' Show me how to love," I prayed with each dish I washed. "Show me how to love," I prayed as I pushed the stroller carrying Heidi and Jared through the dust and potholes to Bloléquin's outdoor market.

God always multi-tasks. I knew I needed to love my friend correctly, but God knew I needed to love the Liberians correctly as well. During our first year of refugee work I became acutely aware I did not love them properly. I deeply resented the lying, shameless begging and the ingratitude. Like Jonah I wanted to die rather than work among them. I actually turned into the "martyr" of 1 Corinthians 13:3: "And though I bestow all my goods to feed the poor, and though I give my body to be burned, but have not love, it profits me nothing."

God knew that now I was ready to be stretched in this area, so He sent me the ultimate test case—Susanna. One day she showed up at my doorstep and though I'd never met her before, without shame or preamble she poured out all of her needs and wants. She spoke in detail of her struggle to parent her five children alone—her husband being trapped in Liberia because of the war.

God was teaching me to love and I certainly didn't want to fail such an obvious test. In fact, I felt God was saying, *If you can love Susanna you can love anyone.* With determination I grabbed my big cloth market bag and ignoring the intense afternoon heat, walked to Bloléquin's market area to buy the items she needed. Later I disturbed Ardith on a Saturday afternoon, asking for medicine for Susanna's baby.

Susanna became a regular at my doorstep. Every few days she came back, asking for more help. People who knew Susanna began warning me things were not as she claimed. Eventually the truth came out. Most obviously, Susanna's husband wasn't trapped in Liberia. He was in town.

Susanna had deceived me. She'd used me. She'd begged constantly and without shame. Truth be told, Susanna encapsulated all the qualities I found most frustrating and irritating. I was tempted to shun her.

The next time Susanna came to my house I confronted her. She sensed her "source of all good things" could dry up, so threw herself at my feet and clutched my ankles. "I hold your foot," she begged in the traditional Liberian manner. Irritated, I shook her off.

If you can love Susanna you can love anyone, God reminded me. I desperately wanted to pass this test, but what did passing the test even look like? I helped her when she needed it. I counseled her regarding family problems she was facing. I encouraged her spiritually. But what did it mean to *love* her?

And so I continued to befriend her. One day, after helping Susanna for several months, she showed up in the yard with a bigger request than usual. "I need money to start a business," she announced with enthusiasm. "If you give it to me, I will never ask you for anything again."

Susanna knew well our house rule about finances. I wasn't to give money without Mark's knowledge and approval. This protected me since I couldn't then be pressured to give away what we needed for personal bills or to a cause Mark felt was not our responsibility. Additionally, it kept the majority of people from asking things from me rather than going directly to him.

"You know I can't give you anything without talking to Mark," I began, and then stopped abruptly as it dawned on me what she was saying. "Are you saying that if I give you this money you will *never* ask me for *anything* again?" I asked eagerly, hope springing up in my heart.

Susanna paused in consternation. Then, with the gusto of one negotiating a great deal with a buyer, she dramatically exclaimed, "Not for two weeks!" I roared with laughter. Susanna joined me. It really was hilarious. We both knew nothing I ever gave her could stop her from asking for more.

I sat on the porch steps feeling somewhat stunned. Susanna was being her usual self and begging shamelessly, but I wasn't irritated. She was trying to "use me," but rather than despising her for it, I found myself amused and unexpectedly sympathetic. God had taught me to love Susanna.

Another regular in our yard was Eugene. We first met him while living in Toulépleu when he responded to a public invitation at the end of a church service. Mark, hearing his slurred speech, thought he was drunk. He found this wasn't the case. Rather Eugene, once a respected schoolteacher, was slowly losing control of his body. As Mark talked with him he felt sadness

The Emptying

for Eugene's physical condition, but was deeply impressed with his faith in God.

Three years later we met Eugene in Bloléquin. He came to our house to ask for help. By now his condition was deplorable. He staggered more than he walked, his dirty legs and feet were covered with dozens and dozens of "jiggers"[1] and rags hung loosely on his thin, weak-looking body. No longer thinking clearly, personal hygiene was forgotten completely. Eugene couldn't always control his bladder so he reeked of stale urine. Rejected by all, he slept in an unfinished house or on a table in the town's open market area.

Loving Eugene was not easy. He was a *lot* of work. Missionaries took turns providing food. Our missionary doctor carefully dug out each of the jiggers—but, unfortunately, not before I found a big jigger burrowed into my own toe. Relatives were located and begged to take responsibility for housing him, but each solution lasted a few weeks at best and then he was back to where he started—a table in the market. It wasn't clear what degenerative disease caused his reduced mental capacity, so the very worst of his problems remained completely unresolved.

One Easter Sunday two young men took Eugene to a bathhouse and scrubbed him until he shone. They dressed him in clean, pressed clothes. Sitting in church, he glowed. Now totally unrecognizable, church members pumped his hand in pleasure and welcomed him as a first-time visitor. To our dismay his clothes were soon stolen and Eugene was back in his stinky, urine-soaked rags. Several months later he died in his sleep on a market table.

Did I pass the "Eugene love test"? I don't know. I did what I could. Was it enough? No, nothing could ever be enough. There was no "enough" in the backwaters of the Ivory Coast. But as a missionary team and a church we did do *something*. Eugene didn't die of starvation or of jiggers. He probably died of the dis-

---

[1] The chigoe flea which burrows into the skin to lay eggs and leave ugly raised sores.

ease causing all of his obvious physical deterioration—whatever that was.

What I learned was this. I wasn't to feel some kind of weird pressure to love a people group; I was to love individuals. I may have been called by God to work among the Liberian people, but love was given to Liberian people one at a time. When I loved Susanna and Eugene I loved as Jesus loved—individually. This clearer understanding of love in real life and practice was tremendously freeing.

At the same time God was teaching me what it really meant to love, He revealed another major root of sin in my life. Lust. Unbelievably, I now understood that the craving I felt for approval wasn't just "my personality," but actually a form of lust. I *lusted* for affirmation. While kneeling in prayer one day God made it clear that He was now asking for my undivided loyalty. I was never to ask for, nor in any other way seek affirmation from anyone but Him again—ever.

But I was an affirmation junkie! Give it up cold turkey? I rocked back from my knees and sank onto the floor, laughing out loud. God knew me *so* well, and it was just like Him to diagnose my exact condition and then prescribe the very medicine I needed—no matter how bitter that medicine tasted.

Only later, telling Mark about the new "rule" in my life—no asking for, or in any other way seeking, affirmation—did I begin to realize the full ramification of this commitment. Mark's praise meant a lot to me, but now I couldn't solicit it. I couldn't ask him, "Do you love me?" The hoped-for (expected!) response was, of course, "Yes, and you're so wonderful," etc., etc., etc. It was seeking affirmation. "Does this dress look good on me?" was an off-limits question if I knew full well it did and simply wanted to hear him say so. No question could be asked unless it was an honest question. No pulling strings to get a compliment.

Many times in the weeks and months following I bit my tongue halfway through a question. "Do you love me?" became, "I love you." "Do you think this looks good?" became, "You look handsome today!" Once in a while I'd start a sentence and

The Emptying

realize I couldn't turn it into anything acceptable. "Oops, I guess I can't ask that," I'd admit guiltily. Mark confessed later he had never liked it when I sought affirmation. Unlike me, he saw no value in a forced complement. Now he felt free to give honest compliments in his own time and in his own way.

This process of sanctification continued in my life as one by one God revealed sinful habits requiring repentance: gossip, anger, bitterness, selfishness, self-righteousness and always more pride. God's grace invited stark, gut-wrenching honesty. And because of His grace He never rejected me.

The whole process was both excruciatingly painful and wonderfully exciting at the same time. I knew that only a very dearly loved child received such close attention from her Father. I now truly and completely believed the real Nancy was safe with this God I was getting to know so intimately and I could now see God was after something big. Something bigger than big. Something huge. My death. My crucifixion with Christ.

On one never-to-be-forgotten Sunday afternoon I was in our bedroom praying and unexpected thoughts filled my mind. God helped me understand what had happened to me. With the exception of my immediate family, one by one God had stripped away every single thing I valued. At first it was the big, obvious things such as possessions, ministries, security and any semblance of control of my life. After that He pried from my grasping fingers my friend, visible "full-time Christian service," and most recently the affirmation of people. The only thing left was nothing. I was absolutely empty.

When you are empty, it is enough, God whispered to my heart.

Oh, wow. At last I understood. Several times during our first term of service in Liberia I'd sobbed in frustration, "It's never enough. Nothing I do is ever enough!" Although I loved being in Liberia and the ministries in which I was involved, I felt I was on a hamster wheel, going around and around. I reasoned, surely if I could do just *one more thing* God's insatiable appetite for my service would be satisfied. He would then love and approve of me.

I'd given God my life in missionary service because I thought it was what He wanted. I understood now that what God had wanted all along was my emptiness. He wanted me totally humble before Him. He wanted me totally aware of my inability to serve Him and to live a life pleasing to Him without His moment-by-moment grace. All Nancy Sheppard had to give God was nothing. Absolutely nothing. But, *When you are empty, it is enough.*

And so I gave my emptiness to God. As I knelt before the bed with my cupped hands lifted, I told God I understood I had nothing to offer Him except my emptiness. But if my emptiness were of use, He could have it all. I asked Him to take the emptied space—the space that used to be filled with so many things I now understood had not been pleasing to Him—and fill it with Himself.

Later I told Mark what I now understood. He could see it was true; God was doing a similar work in his life. What joy we shared. Truly we were partners on this most fascinating journey. Holding my hands in his and lifting them up to God, Mark sang *Treasures,* a song we both knew from our youth but never understood until now.

<u>Treasures</u>
One by one He took them from me,
All the things I valued most,
Until I was empty-handed;
Every glittering toy was lost.

And I walked earth's highways, grieving.
In my rags and poverty.
Till I heard His voice inviting,
"Lift your empty hands to Me!"

So I held my hands toward heaven,
And He filled them with a store
Of His own transcendent riches,

The Emptying

Till they could contain no more.

And at last I comprehended
With my stupid mind and dull,
That God could not pour His riches
Into hands already full![2]

---

[2] Martha Snell Nicholson, "Treasures," Chicago, IL, Moody Press, 1952, pg. 5.

Chapter 10: In Love

I could now see that first awful year of refugee work was necessary; I needed to see who I really was. Everything God had done and was now doing was because of His love. He'd broken me so He could put me back together again. I understood He didn't mean for me to wallow in shame, but rather to believe Romans 8:1. "There is therefore now no condemnation to them which are in Christ Jesus, who walk not after the flesh, but after the Spirit."

God had shown Himself to be a very patient Father as he pointed out my sin and challenged me to become less like me and more like Jesus Christ. My obedience to God's commands

and my repentance of revealed sin—changing wrong thinking to correct, biblical thinking—were the keys unlocking the door to intimacy with God. Much as a parent smiles with joy when his baby crawls, then walks and finally runs, I felt His pleasure in me. I didn't have to win His favor; I already had it. He felt so close I imagined His breath in my ear. After all He had done and was presently doing for me and in me, I no longer doubted that God loved *me*—not my service. But did *I* really love *Him?* I wondered.

One morning in the midst of a busy week of ladies' seminar, I was teaching a lesson about submission. Undistracted by the noises just outside the mud-brick church building, the ladies listened attentively as I explained our responsibility to put ourselves under the authority of our husbands, who must in turn put themselves under the authority of God.

"We must follow the example of Jesus, who submitted to the will of the Father," I explained. As I sometimes do, I dramatized the story of Jesus washing the feet of His disciples to demonstrate the necessity of serving others rather than lording it over them. Kneeling before my friend, I took her foot in my hand and pretended to wash it as Jesus washed His disciples' feet. I choked up. Frustrated with my emotions, I paused and swallowed hard. I was then able to continue with the lesson.

I gave another example of submission—the ultimate example. I told of Jesus' submission to the will of the Father as evidenced by His dying a horribly painful death on a cross. As I spoke tears streamed down my face. My throat filled and I couldn't speak. I had to pause until I could regain my composure.

"Why is this happening to me?" I questioned internally.

You have fallen in love with Jesus, the still, small voice of the Holy Spirit whispered to me.

Yes, I had. How could I expect to tell such precious stories about Jesus without deep emotion? I was in love with Him! Jesus was no longer a taskmaster, but a friend. I now understood and claimed John 15:15—"No longer do I call you servants, for a servant does not know what his master is doing; but I have called you friends, for all things that I heard from My Father I have made known to you." Lord and Master, yes. Also friend and brother.

It was more than I ever dared hope, this amazing love relationship. It was as though God had placed a rope in the palm of my hand and oh-so-tenderly drawn me to Himself. He wooed me as a lover woos his beloved. Friendships and even marriage paled in comparison to the amazing beauty of this intimacy with God. Unwittingly I'd sought from Mark and friends what could in actuality be found only in God—satisfaction in the deepest places of my soul.

After close to two years of emotional separation, my friend and I reconciled. It was wonderful. But because of God's amazing grace poured out on me, by the time our relationship was restored I understood the love of Jesus was better than the love of even the best "people friends."

Chapter 11: Good News

In Liberia and around the world Taylor's exploits made stunning headlines. His seemingly endless supply of guns—M-16s, Tommy Guns, pistols, antiaircraft guns and AK 47s—were used to spread unrestrained terror. He signed multiple peace agreements with, it appeared, no intention of honoring them. While talking peace he prepared for war and when it became apparent he was losing ground, he called for peace.

If ever there was a hopeless and unworkable conclusion to a peace conference, it was 1993's call for the creation of a broad-based Liberian government. In other words, split the government of Liberia among the most powerful warlords in the hope that they'll be placated and stop the killing. If it hadn't been so serious it would have been downright funny. Mortal enemies who had spent the last years trying to kill each other now roamed the same presidential mansion—each surrounded by armed-to-the-teeth bodyguards. A bump in the hall could end in a firefight.

Meanwhile around the country rebel groups remained entrenched. They weren't going to let any power-sharing government interfere with their profiteering. In April of 1996 factional fighting spread to an overpopulated and beleaguered Monrovia, and once again it got very bloody.

By this time all of Liberia was convinced the violence wouldn't stop until Charles Taylor got what he wanted—the presidency. Voters in Monrovia chanted, "You killed my ma, you killed my pa. I'll vote for you." On July 19, 1997, after seven years of madness, they did just that. Charles Taylor won the election fair and square. No other candidate took more than ten percent of the vote.

If Taylor thought his troubles would be over when his title in world circles changed from "warlord Charles Taylor" to "democratically elected President Charles Taylor," he was sorely mistaken. Remnants of multiple rebel factions with thousands of guns were all over the country and these fighters who had shown no respect for the power-sharing government had even less respect for a government where Taylor was on top.

Taylor made attempts at appeasement and incorporated some rival warlords into his new government. Liberia made headline news around the world on September 20, 1998, when warlord-turned-"Rural Development Minister" Roosevelt Johnson feared his life was in danger and sought refuge in the U.S. embassy in Monrovia. Taylor heard of it and his military raced to the site. They killed several of Johnson's supporters in front of the embassy and in the process injured two embassy guards. When Taylor's military fired into the compound itself, presumably in their pursuit of Johnson, the U.S. ambassador reacted immediately and closed the embassy for two months.

Meanwhile in the Ivory Coast our missionary team was going through its own struggles. The physical challenges of living in West Africa were, as always, very great. Besides the daily realities of living among thousands of war torn and impoverished people, malaria and any number of other diseases were a constant threat. In the tropical heat and humidity we suffered with seemingly endless sores and boils. Additionally, the existing French-speaking Ivorian church under which the clinic operated was spiritually weak. There was extreme disunity between the Ivorian and the Liberian believers, causing a constant undercurrent of tension. We knew it wasn't a battle against flesh and blood, but rather it was a spiritual battle. Satan wanted all the ministries to fail and the missionaries to pack up and leave.

When Jeff Abernethy and Mark felt God was leading them to begin an English-speaking church for the refugees in Bloléquin, the Liberians were thrilled. To draw attention to the new work special evangelistic meetings that included gospel videos, music and preaching were held. From the first services Good News Baptist Church was well attended.

Our new church's Wednesday night prayer meetings were very exciting. Often we had eighty or more people in attendance. We made lists of unsaved friends and relatives and then prayed for these people. We saw God answer in a variety of interesting ways. Liberian refugees and their American missionaries alike were learning more about the amazing power of prayer.

Besides Wednesday prayer meeting at church, each Tuesday night our missionary team met for prayer in a home. At one of these meetings I prayed aloud that hundreds of people in our area would come to know Christ as Savior. *Pray for thousands*, God's Spirit prompted.

Organization service of the Good News Baptist Church

Knowing this request lined up with the written Word of God, we wrote our prayer supporters in the U.S. and asked them to join our church and missionary team in prayer. We understood there was nothing we could do to force an answer to this request. Either God was in it or He wasn't.

In July of 1997 Jeff preached a particularly stirring sermon. He told how, after seeing Christ for the first time, Andrew ran to get his brother Peter. Jeff encouraged those who were interested in bringing others to Christ, as Andrew had, to stay after the service. Many stayed behind. These became our core group. Jeff and Kim Abernethy trained some and we the others. They learned the basics of presenting an individual with his or her need of Christ as Savior. Even while still taking the course, several led friends and neighbors to Christ.

After the course was completed "Operation Andrew" began. Each Saturday we went out in small groups, asking God to lead us to those willing and eager to listen. God's Holy Spirit opened their eyes of understanding and many accepted Christ as Savior.

"Reverend Jeff" at Good News Baptist Church

Good News

Our church was vibrant. The excitement spilled over into evangelistic efforts beyond Bloléquin. Through a patient at the clinic God opened up the opportunity for a meeting in a nearby village. While twenty-three people met together to pray, forty-three went with Jeff and Mark to the village. Approximately five hundred people attended the meeting and heard a clear presentation of the gospel.

Each week music poured out of the open windows of the large mud brick church building as believers lifted their voices in praise to the One who had saved them from the war and then saved them from their sins. People grew in their new faith as they listened to the clear teaching from the Word of God. On a regular basis with voices lifted in song, feet shuffling and hands clapping, excited Liberians escorted new believers to the river for baptism.

With awe and amazement I watched God answer our team's prayers for thousands to come to Christ. Participation in such a harvest of souls was a missionary's dream come true. It certainly wasn't because we "deserved" it. Rather, I believe God's blessing was poured out on our missionary team because, though pathetically flawed, we had individually yielded to the flame of the Refiner's fire. To *God* be the glory!

Chapter 12: Patience

"My husband wants to be a missionary, but I won't let him," the pretty young lady stated matter-of-factly.

Her friend nodded, blond hair bobbing in the spring sunshine. "Mine wants to be a missionary too, but I want what's best for my children. I want them to go to the best schools."

While in the United States on home assignment, Mark and I were invited to speak at a Bible college's annual missions conference. I was walking behind two young married students who obviously didn't know I could hear their conversation. Their boldness startled me and I wondered if perhaps I should step back lest a lightening bolt from heaven strike and I get fried along with them!

Though these young women were foolish and bold for saying it aloud, it was in fact what many people were thinking. Only parents unconcerned for their children's best interests took them from the United States and its opportunities.

Yet Africa was home to our children and they truly loved it. They were crazy about animals and sometimes I wondered if our house wasn't more of a zoo than anything else. Giving each animal the most perfect name possible was of utmost importance and often required much discussion. Arnold, Clifford, Leonard, Rebecca and Squirrel Nutkins were just a few of the many pets that shared our quarters.

Occasionally things got a bit out of hand—even by the kids' standards. Melodie's collection of very fertile guinea pigs living in the corner of the yard would receive a regular culling when indoor carnivorous pets such as a genet cat or weasel escaped. There would be the inevitable weeping and wailing and then, when sobbing subsided, the same conversation once again; you can't keep carnivores and their prey on the same yard and not expect trouble from time to time.

The advantages of leaving Minnesota's winters for West Africa's year-'round summer were not lost on our children. While their U.S. counterparts shivered through yet another winter, our children lived on the edge of the jungle and played with children who had never seen a snowflake. They swung from vines into rivers shaded by lush foliage and swam in the Atlantic's warm tropical waters. They'd tasted snail, termite, and the meat of a bizarre variety of animals and were proud of their tolerance for Liberian hot pepper.

Melodie helping at a Bible club

Additionally, our children had wonderful opportunities to be missionaries themselves. At church John-Mark accompanied congregational singing with his guitar. As well as the balafon[1] he bought in the market, he also played the West African kora, mandolin and wooden flute—all of which he made himself. Melodie sang with John-Mark's instrumental and vocal accompaniment. Outside of church John-Mark and Melodie taught children's Bi-

---

[1] African instrument similar to a xylophone.

Patience

ble clubs. Nathan, with his dozens of friends, was great for gathering crowds and helping with games for the clubs others organized.

And like people everywhere, God used my children to grow me.

"I could *never* home school. I'm much too impatient," admirers said when we were in the States. I smiled modestly. What could I say? Was I the only home-school mother with the dirty little secret? The "my children get on my nerves" secret? To my shame, despite God's incredible purifying work in my life I remained impatient with my children.

Nathan especially tried me. It wasn't that he couldn't learn—he was a whiz at anything computer related—he just didn't want to learn. He was a "people lover" and schoolwork wasn't a social activity. I couldn't motivate him to cooperate. I tried everything—a variety of books, a variety of methods, a variety of teaching styles—all to no avail. John-Mark and Melodie made me appear successful as a home-school mother; Nathan toppled that image. He destroyed *my* image. I found it really irritating.

I loved James 1:2-6. It had comforted me immeasurably in the past:

> My brethren, count it all joy when you fall into various trials, knowing that the testing of your faith produces patience. But let patience have its perfect work, that you may be perfect and complete, lacking nothing. If any of you lacks wisdom, let him ask of God, who gives to all liberally and without reproach, and it will be given to him. But let him ask in faith, with no doubting, for he who doubts is like a wave of the sea driven and tossed by the wind.

I knew it was true. The testing of my faith *had* produced patience. I "stuck to the stuff" and stayed in refugee work. As a result I certainly was much more patient than I used to be. But could the testing of my faith produce patience for the seemingly impossible and endless job of schooling this child?

Once again I was ready to be frightfully honest with God. I admitted to Him what He already knew; I was an impatient mother and I resented the very real possibility of public humiliation my lack of home-schooling success presented. I told God I was ready now to call it *sin*. I wanted to change no matter the price and no matter how long it took.

God reminded me of several important principles. The first and most obvious was this: Nathan couldn't *make* me sin; I *chose* to sin. Secondly, when I sinned I must confess it to God and to Nathan. Thirdly, if I recognized sin while it was happening, I could and should ask forgiveness immediately—even mid-sentence. No waiting period necessary.

With this increased transparency I faced my home-schooling responsibilities. I no longer blamed Nathan for my sin. Knowing I had to confess and ask forgiveness helped me to keep my tongue in check. When I did fail I repented to Nathan, who was always more than willing to forgive, and to God. Furthermore, I helped Nathan understand that I couldn't *make* him learn, but if he wanted to graduate from high school and go on to college before we all died of old age he had to complete certain requirements. Clarified expectations and responsibilities freed both of us.

Patience

The sin of impatience had held me tight. Despite my very sincere desire to change, victory was far from instantaneous. At first I committed the same sins each day—sometimes repeatedly. The difference was that now I took full ownership. Gradually, however, I experienced noticeable victory. I'd have one and then two days without being impatient. Then even longer. Eventually the temptation lost its fierce grip on me.

Nathan and I grew closer. He could see I loved him and that I wanted a good relationship with him. And Nathan, being who he is, in a funny kind of way was a bit proud of himself for being such a purifying influence in my life.

I fell more in love with this amazing God who allowed, even desired, unashamed transparency and who was always so ready to forgive. He *knew* my sin of impatience and He also knew I was deadly serious about my repentance. I could be absolutely vulnerable with Him. God was trustworthy.

Chapter 13: Mom

> He who loves father or mother more than Me is not worthy of Me. And he who loves son or daughter more than Me is not worthy of Me. (Matthew 10:37)

We were well aware that God's call on our lives was not without a price. While God had blessed us in countless ways through the years and we were very grateful, there was no getting around the fact that our mission commitment took us far from our extended families. Our children didn't know their relatives nearly as well as I wished and I went years without seeing my twin sister or my parents. Now my mother was diagnosed with a brain tumor and the prognosis was bleak.

Melvin and Ellen Brushaber with Karen, Paul, Dan and Nancy—1964

During our one-year home assignment in 1999, Mom, Karen and I were able to spend some real quality time together in Wisconsin. The three of us played table games, went shopping and ate at some fun restaurants, but mostly we just talked for hours and hours about anything and everything. Karen and I were extremely blessed by Mom's godly attitude about her condition. She wanted to live, but was not afraid to die.

When the time came to set a date for returning to Africa I was in a dilemma. It was unlikely Mom would live until our next home assignment. I knew she wouldn't want me staying in the States waiting for her death, yet I wanted to be with her when she was actually dying. I wanted to say goodbye in person.

We returned to the Ivory Coast on schedule, trusting God to work out the details. It was impossible to make a plan, of course. It could be weeks, months or even a year or two before I was needed in Wisconsin. Mark asked me how long I thought would be necessary for my trip back to the States when the inevitable time arrived. "Three weeks," I said.

Mid-March it happened. Karen called to tell me I needed to get home as soon as possible. She only hoped it wasn't too late. Mom was lying unconscious on the hospital bed set up in the living room. She'd been asleep for more than twenty-four hours. The hospice workers felt death was close.

Mark arranged plane tickets for me as Melodie and I talked about her responsibilities while I was away. The wide diversity of experiences through the years had molded her into a very responsible teen. I knew she'd be able to take care of the meals for the family and, along with John-Mark and Nathan, help Mark care for Heidi and Jared.

As Mark and I drove to the airport three days later it felt very strange. In all of our years in Africa the ocean had never separated us. Now we were saying good-bye to each other and hello to a lot of unknowns. Yet I felt great peace. God was in complete control and I knew it.

Please give me a seat by myself, I prayed as I boarded the airplane. I was feeling subdued and didn't want to explain to a stranger why I was flying internationally. I sat alone. And then in Brussels I prayed the same thing as I stood in line with the large crowd of boarding passengers. Only one seat on the plane was empty. It was next to me.

My brother Peter met me in Chicago. While it was wonderful to see him again, excitement over our reunion was, of course, diminished by our shared concern. Although she'd briefly awakened after Karen's original phone call to me, Mom was once again in a deep and prolonged sleep. She was expected to die at any moment.

When we arrived in Whitewater my dad and Karen met us at the door. Mom was still unconscious but not dead, they reported. I was very happy and relieved. "This is *not* what God brought me home for," I said to Karen after we hugged each other. I knew Mom would wake up again.

And she did. That evening. When Mom's eyes opened and she saw me, her face lit up. Too weak to move but not in pain, Mom smiled with joy as Karen and I talked and laughed and joked. She whispered her comments and we cherished them like precious jewels. Mom loved music so Karen and I opened the hymnbook and, starting with page one, sang every song we knew—which was a lot of them—as she lay on her hospice bed with a look of complete contentment. This fun spirit continued day after day. Mom would sleep for many hours and then, there she was, ready for more singing and laughing and joking.

Mom wasn't afraid to talk about her condition, so there was no reason to be guarded. "You need a head transplant," we teased.

Without skipping a beat she whispered back, "I don't want just any head. It has to be a pretty one!"

God allowed us more than a week. Finally the day came we knew was the last she would wake. Though incredibly weak and unable to speak, Mom was aware. We gathered around, saying our last earthly goodbyes. We thanked her for everything, told her of our love and sent messages to heaven with her. "Tell Grandma Hansen we love her! Tell her we'll be coming!"

The next day, after many hours of deep sleep, Mom's breathing became very labored. We knew death was extremely close.

But we knew that this wasn't only a death; this was actually also a birth—a birth into eternal life.

We knew Mom would want music around her as she died. Others gathered near while, sitting one on each side of her, Karen and I sang, "Jesus, I am Resting," "My Faith has Found a Resting Place" and "Draw Me Nearer." And then lastly, as she entered the presence of God, "My Jesus, I Love Thee."

> <u>My Jesus, I Love Thee</u>
> My Jesus, I love Thee, I know Thou art mine;
> For Thee, all the follies of sin I resign;
> My gracious Redeemer, My Savior art Thou;
> If ever I loved Thee, my Jesus, 'tis now.
>
> I love Thee because Thou hast first loved me,
> And purchased my pardon on Calvary's tree;
> I love Thee for wearing the thorns on Thy brow;
> If ever I loved Thee, my Jesus, 'tis now.
>
> I will love Thee in life, I will love Thee in death,
> And praise Thee as long as Thou lendest me breath;
> And say, when the death-dew lies cold on my brow;
> "If ever I loved Thee, my Jesus, 'tis now."
>
> In mansions of glory and endless delight,
> I'll ever adore Thee in heaven so bright;
> And singing Thy praises, before Thee I'll bow;
> If ever I loved Thee, my Jesus, 'tis now. [1]

I completely expected to see angels. I could feel them in the room.

Mom's entrance into heaven was April 6, 2000. Karen and I were born April 8, 1960. In other words, we were together and we were turning forty. Unfortunately, with Mom's recent death it was difficult to know how much celebrating was appropriate. Yet it seemed wrong not to celebrate. After all, *Mom* had considered

---

[1] William Featherston, "My Jesus, I Love Thee" (1864). Music: Adoniram Gordon, 1876.

our birthday a great day! Then, completely unexpectedly, a party came to us. One after another friends and relatives came bringing a cake, balloons, cards, gifts and most importantly themselves, making an important but awkward birthday very, very special.

Mom always loved an occasion—and her funeral was an occasion! It was two days after our birthday and, filled with meaningful songs, heartfelt eulogies and an abundance of red roses, it was beautiful.

After the funeral I concentrated on preparing for my return to Africa. I ran the errands I needed to run, bought what needed to be bought, and visited the people whom I needed to visit.

Then I flew back to Africa, another passenger next to me on each leg of the journey with whom I shared the story of God's goodness. I arrived back home three weeks after I left—exactly the amount of time I'd told Mark I would need.

I learned God was as real in death as He is in life. Everything Mom needed in life God had provided. Everything she needed in death He had also provided. Everything I needed, and some things I simply wanted, God provided for me as well.

Chapter 14: The Making of a Man

"Mark! Look at this! You're rich—and getting richer every day!"

I was reading in the sixth chapter of the book of Luke. Verses twenty-two and twenty-three jumped out at me:

> Blessed are you when men hate you,
> And when they exclude you,
> And revile you, and cast out your name as evil,
> For the Son of Man's sake.
> Rejoice in that day and leap for joy!
> For indeed your reward is great in heaven,
> For in like manner their fathers did to the prophets.

We knew the Liberian Civil War was at our doorstep, but another kind of war—an immense spiritual battle—was being fought as well.

Missionaries with a variety of denominations and organizations had ministered for decades in Liberia. Baptist Mid-Missions sent its first couple in 1938. More than one hundred BMM missionaries had lived and worked in Liberia since then. The missionaries were given land grants on which to build churches or mission stations, and in the earlier days of mission work in Liberia, because the Americo-Liberians in government focused most of their attention on coastal cities, no roads led to these properties. The missionaries walked. No houses, water wells or electric generators waited for these pioneers.

Their message was simple and amazing: Jesus Christ, God's beloved Son, was sent from heaven to earth. His earthly mother Mary was a virgin at His conception. After living a perfect life Jesus was cruelly crucified on a Roman cross, was buried, and then rose from the grave the third day, victorious over death. This proved once and for all Jesus' claim that He was God, "I and my Father are one" (John 10:30), and that His death, rather than simply a cruel fate, was preplanned and had massive supernatural significance. Jesus had given Himself as a gift, the atoning sacrifice God's holiness demanded for the sins of mankind. To become a child of God, a Christian, one must repent of sin and acknowledge Jesus as lord and master. To do this meant to accept the most amazing gift possible—eternal life with God Himself in heaven.

Some received this good news gladly and in a flurry of excitement missionaries created schools so new converts to Christianity could learn to read the Bible. After all, reading was the key to understanding God's written instructions for the Christian life. Even though officially the English brought by the Americo-Liberians was the national language, until this time many Liberians in the interior of the country spoke only their regional dialects. These new mission schools focused much effort on teaching students not only to speak English, but also how to read and write it. This emphasis opened doors of opportunity previously closed to the interior people.

In addition to the schools, mission organizations also opened clinics and hospitals. Not surprisingly, wonderful and needed as these ministries were, the tail soon wagged the dog and the original missionary focus of evangelization and discipleship was lost. Rather than prioritizing the spiritual needs of patients, most medical facilities focused primarily on the urgent physical needs. The focus of most schools was no longer reading for the purpose of understanding the Bible, but rather personal advancement. Liberians aligned themselves with the mission group that seemed to offer the best possible present and future benefits.

Then the war came. Foreign missionaries fled and, for the first time in many organizations, Liberians were alone and in charge. Some of the Liberians in key leadership positions had already been proven faithful. Others were thrown into positions of responsibility for the first time as missionaries were running out the door. Because of the urgent needs of the Liberian people and the generosity of those hearing of the needs, agencies sent money to these leaders. Sometimes lots of money.

The Making of a Man

Now, several years into the conflict, many of the Liberian church leaders within the Baptist Mid-Missions fellowship were extremely dissatisfied. In the years since the war started they'd watched many people benefit financially and otherwise from close association with overseas Christian agencies and they felt the benefits of being associated with Baptist Mid-Missions and its missionaries were extremely inadequate. Cars, trips to the States and monthly financial support were just a few of the bigger benefits they'd seen others attain and for which they aspired. Their excellent educations were obvious; they were nothing if not articulate in expressing their dissatisfaction. In fact, both verbally and in writing, these leaders declared the mission's work in Liberia a failure.

In multiple meetings and letters Mark, along with our missionary coworkers, explained the position of our mission board. While we tried to help where we could—hundreds of thousands of dollars had been spent in Liberia through the years on any number of things—the mission's primary goal was not material. Rather, the goal of Baptist Mid-Missions was totally independent, self-sustaining, self-governing ministries. We were committed to this viewpoint. We felt it biblical and had found it successful as well. Throughout Liberia, despite the war, the churches associated with Baptist Mid-Missions had kept their doors open. Other denominations that taught their leaders to depend on outside support had been closed up when the money failed to reach them.

Explanations like this didn't placate these leaders. It became increasingly obvious to us, as first months and then years passed, that they believed if they banded together and were immovable, they could force Baptist Mid-Missions to give in to their demands. Sadly, we realized that for these men Baptist Mid-Missions truly *had* failed. Only people who didn't understand the transcendent value of the gospel could "go on strike" because they'd not been given "stuff."

One particular letter, signed by many Liberian pastors, detailed Baptist Mid-Missions' "failures" dating back more than fifty years. The letter's galling display of ingratitude for the sacrifices of past missionaries was beyond hurtful to both our missionary coworkers and us. These pioneer missionaries were our heroes; for some they were parents, literally. The critical attitude of the spiritually rich, "reached" Liberian leadership contrasted sharply with the needs of the spiritual poor, "unreached" masses in the Ivory Coast. Four missionary families decided to switch their ministry focus from Liberia to the Ivory Coast.

We alone remained. While we understood completely the reasoning of our missionary friends, we couldn't join them. Mark was working closely with several Liberian pastors who thought very differently than those who signed the letter. He felt strongly that God wanted us to encourage these men by continuing our work with them.

Things changed for us when our missionary friends switched their ministry focus. Previous attacks against Baptist Mid-Missions were addressed to the group and answered by the group. Now, because we alone remained officially with Liberia, the complaints came straight to us and the accusations were often personal.

The intensity of the assault drove both of us to prayer and to the Bible. Countless times we threw ourselves on the mercy of God, begging Him to carry this load that was much too great for us to bear. Countless times He raised us up to continue in the grace given for one more day. The Psalms became a living book, breathing hope into us when it seemed all hope was lost. Our enemies were chasing us just as David's enemies had chased him. God had proven Himself faithful to David and surely He would also prove Himself faithful to us. The New Testament was filled with treasures too. We clung to such verses as Hebrew 6:10, "For God is not unjust to forget your work and labor of love which you have shown toward His name, in that you have ministered to the saints, and do minister." We placed ourselves in God's care, knowing that even if everyone else forgot our "labor of love," God would not forget.

The Making of a Man

While we both dealt daily with the fierce attack of those who made themselves our enemies, it was primarily against Mark that the barbs were thrown. The strategy of our detractors was obvious—if they couldn't get Mark to give in to their demands, they could make him so miserable that he quit. At that point they could legitimately say that no one was working with them and pursue a relationship with a new and better organization—one with more benefits.

In a two-day "roast" before a packed church, called under the guise of "solving the problems between us," Mark was accused of a multitude of things, large and small. The Bible school was substandard and he made false claims about it. He associated with bad people. He didn't give enough. It went on and on and on; his detractors were bent on discouraging and defeating him. But rather than being beaten, Mark inwardly chuckled. Who better than he to be in this unenviable position? He was accustomed to trouble! And how ironic that after all of his indiscretions, pranks, and general naughtiness in childhood and young adulthood, here he was, in the worst confrontation of his entire life—worse by far than any trip to the principal's office—and actually *not* guilty!

During the meeting a pastor friend overheard some women surmising that Mark didn't know enough Liberian English to understand what was being said about him. Surely, they reasoned, if he understood what was being said he'd fight his accusers.

No, he understood clearly. But by God's grace Mark was the man for this job. He was very even-tempered and in a situation where other men would explode in anger, Mark sat politely waiting for the appropriate time to speak and God's help to speak in the proper manner. Where other men would be driven by their pride to defend themselves—even while knowing it wouldn't do a bit of good—God had so humbled Mark through our trials that he was now content to let God defend him. Additionally, for eight years Mark had been creating notes for the Bible schools. He'd spent hundreds of hours studying the Bible in his efforts to make these notes as accurate as possible. This "seminary education without actually going to seminary" stood him in good stead. Mark knew how to answer his accusers biblically.

The grown son of a pastor, a man whom we'd thought a friend, confronted Mark as he left the church building when the first day ended. Didn't Mark consider himself a false prophet? he asked acridly. On the second day, after many more hours of being accused of any number of things, Mark was more than ready to return home. But instead of being allowed to go, he was greeted at the back door of the church by a government official and eventually escorted to the Department of Immigration in Monrovia—in our vehicle and at our expense. He was accused of coming into Liberia illegally. Much more seriously—potentially even deadly—he'd also been accused of being a mercenary. Thankfully officials were too embarrassed by the ridiculousness of the charge to press it. After Mark explained to the Bureau of Immigration official where he'd just come from and what was happening, the man was able to see through the accusations to what lay behind them. Mark was released to return to the Ivory Coast.[1]

In the continued heat of the Refiner's fire I watched Mark grow. *Who is this man who loves the Bible so much?* I asked myself as he stood in front of a group of pastors wisely sharing God's Word. *Who is this man who delights in seeing people grow in their faith?* I wondered as he walked into the river to baptize Liberian believers. *Who is this man who counsels our children so wisely? Who is this man who is so radical about inward purity?* He was certainly not the Mark Sheppard I married. He was also not any product of nit-picking, hen-pecking or fix-up efforts on my part. No, this Mark Sheppard was someone only God could have made.

---

[1] 2010 update: after dealing with this problem for many years, upon our return to Liberia in 2004 a delegation came to smooth over the problem. Mark and other pastors have had several meetings with them in the years following. The church fellowships are now moving closer to true, Christ-honoring reconciliation.

The Making of a Man

Mark leads the rejoicing after a baptism service

Chapter 15: Becoming Sarah's Daughter

Mark and I were both growing and changing and were living within our marriage in more harmony than ever before. We both became more transparent about our faults and were quicker to acknowledge our sins. Though we were certainly not sinless, we were sinning less and less.

Through the years I'd read dozens, if not hundreds, of Christian books on the subject of marriage and the home. I regularly taught many women the biblical principles in groups and one on one. To be honest, I thought I pretty much knew all the Bible had to say about marriage and being a good wife.

Then one day while reading my Bible, God pierced my heart with 1 Peter 3:5-6. "For in this manner, in former times, the holy women who trusted in God also adorned themselves, being submissive to their own husbands, as Sarah obeyed Abraham, calling him lord, whose daughters you are if you do good and are not afraid with any terror." Over the next several days I found myself reading and rereading the verses in several Bible translations. I began to wonder why I kept thinking about them and what the passage could possibly have to do with me.

Obviously Sarah really respected Abraham a lot if she referred to him as "lord" and obviously that lord-talk honored God enough to point it out—even say that women could become Sarah's daughters by imitating her and by not giving in to any fear. I knew Ephesians 5:33 in the King James Version of the Bible said that the wife should "see that she reverence her husband," and wondered if these two passages were talking about the same thing. Was this extreme respect that Sarah showed for Abraham an example of biblical reverence?

After several days of reading and rereading the verses and thinking a good deal about them, I was forced to acknowledge that God Himself was the source of my obsession. Obviously there was something in these verses He wanted me to notice. Something He wanted me to obey. But what?

Was God asking me to *reverence* Mark?

Surely, surely, *surely* I was misunderstanding something. As politically incorrect as submission sounded and actually was—and I was the first to acknowledge that it certainly didn't pass a single political correctness test—reverence was *much* worse! Besides, wasn't reverence something reserved for God, Who was great, holy and perfect? He deserved it! But reverence a person? Reverence *Mark*? Changing and growing though he was, he wasn't perfect and reverencing him seemed a bit over the top, to say the least! Besides, did Mark even *want* to be reverenced?

On the other hand, I didn't want to miss anything God had for me and He'd certainly not led me astray in any other area! What if there was another level of obedience to God that asked I go beyond the submission I was practicing and actually reverence Mark?

Finally I talked to him. I wanted Mark's assurance the passage wasn't asking for anything new. Opening my Bible, I jabbed a finger at 1 Peter: 3:6. "How does this apply to me?" I asked. "Submission *is* reverence, right? Or at least close enough? It can't mean what it looks like it means! Besides, do you even *want* this?" Wisely Mark didn't answer and instead left the room to look up the passage in various Bible study aids. He knew this had nothing to do with what he wanted or didn't want.

"Besides, I'm not afraid of anything!" I called after him.

You are afraid. You are afraid Mark will take it to be "small."

I was shocked by the sudden truth that flooded my thoughts. I realized that indeed I *was* afraid! I was afraid that if I did this—*reverenced* Mark—that he'd think it was something he simply deserved or, more galling yet, that somehow this was easy for me and therefore almost insignificant. Something small. No, this was *huge!*

Mark returned from the office. "It's as bad as it looks," he said. 'Submission and reverence are not the same thing." He told me that to submit meant, "to yield to one's admonition or advice." Reverence meant, "to treat with deference or reverential obedience."

Well, God knew if I gave Mark reverence—took it up to *that* level—it had to be because God Himself was asking it of me. Yet I could see from I Peter 3:5-6 that it *was* God, and not Mark, asking for it.

"O.K. Then I'll *do* it!" I announced heatedly.

In the days following this surrender I spent a lot of time thinking of what reverence could possibly look like when fleshed out in daily life. Calling Mark "lord" was obviously not the 21st-century answer. No, it wasn't a title God was asking me to give Mark, but rather I was to defer to him with reverence. Real respect.

So with God's help, I did it. Not flawlessly by any means, but I upped the respect. And with this surrender something unexpected happened. Mark totally relaxed in our relationship. In an odd way it was almost visible physically. One day he confessed, "In the past I knew you were trying, but I always feared the old Nancy would rise up and challenge me. Now I believe you." I hadn't realized he too had fears. I was thankful my commitment was made verbally.

Mark fell more deeply in love with me, perhaps because there was a new level of trust between us. With eyes filled with love he told me how blessed he was to have me. He followed me around talking to me—wanting to touch me. It was like a honeymoon thing!

And even as I sought to treat Mark with this new level of respect, I enjoyed my secret. While the world would have women believe they were strong when they forced their will on others, I knew the truth. Reverencing another human being took *much* greater strength than pushing for my own way.

Mark certainly did not take it to be "small," as I feared he would. He knew me too well for that! He'd witnessed the struggle and knew this surrender was yet another death to self. I was so very glad I'd yielded to the authority of God's Word. I saw once again that when God asked something of me, He always had my very best interest at heart.

Chapter 16: Tested by Fire

"People over here aren't buying what you're selling," Karen replied when I told her the lessons God was teaching me about reverence. I chuckled inwardly.

In San Pedro, the coastal city in which we were now living, we had access to e-mail. My twin sister and I were enjoying something we never dreamed possible—regular contact even though I was in Africa. We discussed anything and everything. Since we were twins, I was especially intrigued with God's work in her life and any parallels with His work in my life. Were these lessons God was teaching me through refugee work universal? If so, how would God teach Karen?

Karen told me about her church and all the things her family was learning. Her pastor was preaching a series of sermons on *The Treasure Principle*. Using the principles stated in Randy Alcorn's small book by the same title, the congregation was being encouraged to trust God with their finances. And then at a mission conference the speaker incorporated the same theme. If unexpected money came in, would you be willing to give it to God?, he challenged.

One day Karen wrote me an especially exciting letter. Completely out of the blue money from a lawsuit between former employee-shareholders and her husband's former employer became available. Rather than building a desperately needed addition to their small house, they were giving the money to God as promised. Specifically, it was being used to fund summer mission trips for Karen and her children. Thirteen-year-old Kiersten was going to Ethiopia and seventeen-year-old Chip to Malawi. Karen, with baby Jake, was coming to the Ivory Coast.

It was a dream come true! Karen was visiting me in Africa. But she must work, she said. It couldn't be just for pleasure. It was to be a real mission trip. With enthusiasm I planned our projects. In the States Karen packed and got Jake caught up on his vaccinations, ready for travel.

I was beside myself with excitement the day Karen and Jake arrived. I couldn't wait to show off the Ivory Coast. My missionary life had always been such a mystery to her and now, at last, Karen would experience it for herself.

It was interesting to see Abidjan through her eyes. We were used to seeing the thousands of pedestrians who dashed madly through traffic at rush hour, but she wasn't. We had seen the shanties that stood impossibly close together in the slums or were built against the wall of an opulent compound. And the "walking Wal-Mart" vendors, those fearless men who ran into the intersections at red lights selling everything from ironing boards to parrots, no longer startled us. But they sure startled Karen!

Nancy and Karen in San Pedro—2002

Once in San Pedro we began one of our projects—organizing the Bible School library. As Karen and I walked from the school to a small restaurant for lunch, she snapped pictures of scrawny chickens scratching the sides of garbage mountains. Pedestrians laughed with us at Karen's surprise when a herd of gaunt, humped-backed cows sauntered into the road, stalling the busy traffic. Back at the house we interspersed work with play. It was wonderful. And Jake was no problem. Although he was almost one year old, he was extremely passive and just sat still or slept.

Because Karen and I were apart most of the time, she didn't know my children well and I relished this opportunity for her to get to see the beautiful young people they were becoming. John-Mark was away at college, but the other four were there. Melodie cooked delicious meals for us. Nathan charmed Karen with stories of biking mishaps and adventures at the beach. Heidi blessed her with art projects while Jared showed off his favorite toys. The children regaled her with stories of ministry opportunities, social and cultural blunders, and the never-ending string of marriage proposals. We laughed until we cried. While we visited the pet mongoose, palm civet and genet cat—Mr. Anderson, Angie and Alex—romped. Karen was amazed we took for granted zoo animals living in our house.

One week into the trip Karen received an e-mail letter from her husband. "Don't worry about anything," it began. "The fire damage can be fixed up before you get home." It went on to say that the children were fine; they'd jumped out of a window. And then, "What color do you prefer for the new kitchen cabinets?"

What? Fire damage? And if the fire was small and nothing to worry about, why were children jumping out of the window? What was going on! Karen, who knew Chuck liked to break bad news slowly, was suspicious. She wrote a letter asking for details and the next day we eagerly hovered over the computer when we saw a reply had arrived.

"Forget what I said yesterday," Chuck began, and then he went on to tell a more complete version of what had happened and was presently happening. While at the insurance office making a claim, he received a phone call. The original large kitchen fire, put out by the local fire service, had ignited once again and flames were seen leaping out of all the windows of the house when friends drove by.

Karen was distraught. Here she was on the other side of the world while her family was going through this awful trauma. She would have been in Tennessee with them right now if Chuck and she hadn't decided to trust God with their finances. What should she do? Go home? Where was God in all of this? What was He *doing*!

Somewhat humorously, Karen didn't feel the least sorrow about losing the house itself. It was very small for her family of seven. The fact that it was completely paid off had made her husband reluctant to even consider moving. Recently, after years of struggling with her dissatisfaction, Karen had yielded the house situation to God and quit begging to move. Now, because of this fire, they *had* to move. But to where were they moving? A trailer? A house smaller than the one they just lost?

I understood. I knew what it was like to need a house desperately and sought to assure Karen. "I've seen God do this," I said. "Before we went to Bloléquin Mark made a survey trip to look for housing. There was absolutely nothing available meeting our needs and he returned to Abidjan with the bad news.

"Our guest housing in Abidjan expired and we needed to leave. As we were traveling down the road I was thinking of our dilemma. Besides the living and sleeping space for our family of seven, we needed an office and a schoolroom. The house had to be big enough to provide privacy for the overnight guests we hosted from time to time. We really needed a six-bedroom house and the Abernethy family needed the same. There was no such thing in Bloléquin, I knew.

"Then an idea popped into my head. By placing a door between them, we could modify two small apartments to make one large apartment. I described it to Mark as he drove.

"The next day we went searching. On the edge of an overgrown field we found a two-story, unfinished fourplex. It was designed in such a way that it was possible to do exactly as I'd described the day before. Abernethys put a door between the two upper apartments and we did the same with the two downstairs apartments. It worked out perfectly.

"So God is able to do the same for you. He can help Chuck and you find the perfect house for your family. You're here because you trusted God and it's God that will look bad if He doesn't work this out for good in your lives. God can always be trusted to protect His own good name. So, describe to me the house you need for the ministry God has called you to do and I'll write it down."

We sat together at the table and she did just that. Karen began hesitantly, but eventually ideas flowed. She described the house suitable for the needs of her large family. I wrote twelve items—everything from yard size to number of bedrooms. I encouraged her to trust God. I knew He was totally trustworthy.

Two days after her return to Tennessee Chuck and Karen met with a realtor. They described the house they needed. Nothing. Disappointed, they left the office and headed to the burned house to take a look. Later, on the way back to their motel, they noticed a sign in front of a large, red brick house on Main Street. "For Sale by Owner," it read. The house was beautiful and in a nice neighborhood. Pulling over, they got out of the car and peered into the front window. Its interior was open and spacious.

The next day the owner showed them the house. It was everything on the list Karen had dictated to me, plus some. As Karen sent pictures through the Internet and told me more and more details of the house, I knew this was a God-thing.

Although not able to be there in person because we were in Africa, we, nevertheless, rejoiced with Karen the day they moved into the house and again the day they dedicated it to God with an Open House party for family and friends. Such an exciting event merited a special gift. Melodie, Miss Creativity, designed a large cross-stitched project that she and I made together and sent to Tennessee. Above a cornucopia of gorgeous flowers was stitched the key verse from *The Treasure Principle*. "Again, the kingdom of heaven is like treasure hidden in a field, which a man found and hid; and for joy over it he goes and sells all that he has and buys that field. Matthew 13:44." It described perfectly what Chuck and Karen were learning. When you've found the real Treasure, you can trust Him with earthly treasure.

Through the provision of this house Karen saw God's incredible and personal love for her. He gave Karen beyond what she could ask or think (Ephesians 3:20). She needed the lesson. It was foundational for what would come later—Jake's diagnosis of autism. God was doing in Karen's regular, non-missionary life the same purifying work He was doing in my missionary-to-Africa life. It was what He wanted to do in everyone's life.

Chapter 17: Back at Last

In 2001 after a year of living and ministering in San Pedro, Ivory Coast, Mark felt God was leading him to make teaching trips into Liberia. He was deeply burdened for the churches and dreamed of a program that would allow pastors and other church leaders to increase their biblical understanding without excessive time away from their ministries and homes.

Our pastor friends were extremely grateful for Mark's willingness and Baptist Mid-Missions' permission for us to travel from the Ivory Coast into a very insecure Liberia. They loved the Word of God and they loved us. Our hearts were warmed as they effused, "You are better than one hundred missionaries to us. Your hearts are really with us." We were equally thankful for them.

After much planning and preparation, Mark's dream became reality. We flopped from side to side like rag dolls as the Nissan Patrol inched over Liberia's severely potholed roads. In the rainy season we carried a winch to pull ourselves out of the gigantic mud bogs we encountered. Dozens of government checkpoints, sometimes one on each end of a bridge, slowed our travel and tested our patience. Pastors and church leaders came from their towns and villages, some walking for days. For two weeks, eight hours a day, Mark taught until his throat was raw. I taught the women each afternoon after they were finished with their cooking responsibilities.

After one such conference we headed to Monrovia for an important meeting. Upon arrival we learned the meeting was postponed. We booked more days in the guesthouse and decided to make the most of the extra time in Liberia.

The day before our revised departure date Mark flipped on the radio to BBC's *Focus on Africa*. Through the years it had become our habit to listen every day. This kept us abreast of Liberia's news, which was often the headline story. However, to our surprise, the lead story that day was coming not out of Liberia, but instead the Ivory Coast. And the news was dreadful. Disgruntled soldiers were mutinying. Abidjan and several other major cities were under siege. The Ivory Coast was in a state of chaos.

We were stunned, but we shouldn't have been. Violence in the Ivory Coast wasn't new and, given our past experiences, we should've seen it coming. Ever since our first days in refugee work things had been tense. Even before their long-term president Felix Houphouët-Boigny died in 1993 at age 88, the scramble for power had begun in earnest. The relatively peaceful election that followed his death belied the violent undercurrents.

Just before Christmas in 1999 there had been a major coup. A general of the Ivorian military had seized power, accusing the president of financial mismanagement and widespread corruption. The city of Abidjan went crazy, in part because thousands of prisoners were set free. Mark, visiting on business, was leaving just as army troops raced through the city, shooting into the air and seizing vehicles.

Because the elected president had been wildly unpopular, when the general declared himself head of state, people accepted it. Besides, he'd clearly stated that the free and fair election of a new president was his primary objective. However, after enjoying the accolades and many financial perks of presidential life, he changed his mind. When election day arrived and it became evident the people had chosen someone other than him as president, the general refused to accept it and instead declared himself the victor. The people were neither surprised nor fooled. Tens of thousands of Ivorians took to the streets in protest. The gendarmes and police did nothing to stop it, and the military was completely overwhelmed. Demonstrations continued all over the Ivory Coast until the dethroned general disappeared into the interior of the country and the newly elected president claimed his rightful place.

But sadly the problems weren't over. When another party's candidate called upon his supporters to protest the election results and demand new elections, thousands of his supporters took to the streets and hundreds of people were wounded or killed. Eventually order was restored, but the underlying problem remained unresolved.

While democratic elections produced presidents they couldn't force opposition leaders to accept them, so the Ivory Coast seemed always on the verge of yet another uprising. In fact, several months before we'd driven through a huge and potentially violent crowd of political activists while taking my sister to the airport. "Smile and pretend you agree with them," Mark advised as people surged into the road and pounded on our SUV. We gave our best smiles, thumbs ups and waves. Never was Karen so thrilled to see an airport.

Whatever calm existed was shattered on September 19, 2002, when soldiers mutinied and attempted a takeover of the government. Within hours the entire country was under siege. From our Monrovia guesthouse Mark called the Ivory Coast, desperate to find out what was going on. We were informed our missionary friends in Bouaké were trapped in their home as bullets flew over their rooftop. At the nearby missionary boarding school hundreds of children were likewise trapped between warring factions.

The Liberian refugees in the Ivory Coast with whom we had worked for the last thirteen years were caught between a rock and a hard place. The Ivory Coast could easily disintegrate into its own long and drawn-out civil war. Should they stay? Was it time to return to Liberia? The answer was by no means obvious.

Mark and I talked in awed voices of what was becoming increasingly clear. After years of telling our supporting churches, our Liberian friends and our missionary coworkers that we would one day live and work inside Liberia again, we were now being given the chance to do just that.

As the door to the Ivory Coast had closed, God opened up a window for us in Liberia. It was impossible not to see God's hand in the timing. Close to thirteen years after the first shots of

Liberia's civil war were fired, on what we assumed was simply a short trip into Liberia, God had not only protected us from the trauma of an evacuation, He'd actually brought us home.

Chapter 18: The Trap Closes

"The time has come to ask yourself, 'What am I doing here?'" the U.S. ambassador to Liberia said with no hint of humor. He wasn't trying to be dramatic; he was trying to motivate. Unbelievably, after thirteen years in exile we were living in Liberia again. Not quite so unbelievably, we were being urged to leave.

It was February of 2003 and we were sitting on the beautiful beach-front patio of the ambassador's home with more than one hundred other American and foreign nationals. We listened as he matter-of-factly outlined the sad facts of life. Liberia was going downhill fast and this time, because of the Second Gulf War, there would be no U.S. ships with marines offshore to rescue anyone. There would be no sleeping at the embassy compound. There would be no helicopter evacuations. Just go. Leave while you can.

Despite the Ambassador's blunt talk filled with stark realities, we couldn't help but be glad we were back in Liberia. With us for this wild ride was Kim Marks, a short-term missionary volunteer who had traveled with us from the Ivory Coast, never dreaming it would turn into such an adventure. We rented a three-bedroom house on the outskirts of Monrovia that we furnished with what we could borrow or buy cheaply in the market. It felt like camping.

When we went into town a multitude of destitute people clamored for our attention. "My frien'! My frien'! Where my Chris'mas?" "Where my Sataday?" "My weeken' on you-o!" Beggars, some missing multiple limbs, hobbled down the streets through the moonscape of potholes to reach us.

Monrovia, never particularly glorious, was reduced to varying shades of gray. Gray cement buildings crumbled. Gray light posts tilted side-ways, weakened from thousands of bullet holes. Children, gray with dirt, played with pieces of garbage. Gray. Gray. Gray. The whole city was gray. Or so it seemed.

People displaced from their upcountry homes squatted in the houses abandoned by those who had fled to others countries. Large extended families lived together in gutted multi-level buildings in the city center. These buildings' outside walls, where there were walls, were made of either cardboard or old roofing materials. It wasn't unusual for babies to tumble to their deaths.

Dilapidated vehicles, overflowing with passengers, crawled crablike down the streets where filthy, vacant-eyed ex-combatants sauntered unconcerned, shouting nonsense. Police stopped drivers for real and made-up offenses. Military checkpoints slowed traffic to a crawl, with the exception of the trucks of government soldiers who, camouflaged with leafy bushes, raced noisily through the city.

Nightlife was all but nonexistent. Without streetlights—the electric system long gone—the nights were black and dangerous. Men out after dark took the very real risk of being forcibly conscripted into the Liberian army.

Taylor's power was clearly in the decline. People both resented and feared him. Stupidly, while the citizens lived in abject poverty Taylor didn't bother to hide the fact that he was amassing huge wealth. The SIM cards needed in mobile phones sold for $65. More than half of it was for Taylor—not his government, but Taylor personally. Trucks loaded with huge mahogany logs worth tens of thousands of dollars each bumped along dirt highways deep in the interior, heading for Liberia's ports. All profits went straight to Taylor. And unbelievably, while he amassed his enormous fortune, Taylor didn't bother to pay his military. He obviously felt their loyalty was guaranteed.

The nepotism Taylor despised in the previous government was repeated in his own—sometimes on levels that were downright hilarious. For example, it was illegal to import ice cream. Why? Because Taylor's sister was making and selling ice cream and the ban on imports forced everyone to buy hers. On one memorable day, our Lebanese merchant-friend handed us a partially eaten half-gallon, wrapped carefully in a dark plastic bag, so we too could enjoy a taste of the contraband.

Rumor on the street said that Taylor was totally paranoid. So afraid of being poisoned like a past president of Nigeria, he wouldn't eat fresh fruit. So afraid one of his scores of enemies would shoot him, he rarely went out in public.

In the interior of Liberia large tracts of no-man's-land teemed with rebel factions who hated Taylor and coveted his access to wealth. Streams of people were fleeing the chaos created by these groups that specialized in looting, raping and killing. They joined the multitudes in Monrovia, squeezing into the already over-crowded shacks or joining the squatters already ensconced in one of the hundreds of abandoned buildings.

At the same time Taylor had been wreaking havoc in Liberia he apparently had been doing the same in Liberia's neighboring countries. Ironically, rather than Liberia, it was The Special Court for Sierra Leone that charged Taylor with crimes against humanity in 2003. Taylor, they claimed, had armed and trained Sierra Leone's rebels. These brutal warriors ravaged their country, chopping off baby's heads and other civilians' hands—everyone should "give a hand" to the war effort—to terrorize them into fleeing their diamond-rich land. In addition to Sierra Leone, Taylor was also accused of destabilizing Guinea and the Ivory Coast. Blood diamonds. Blood timber. Blood everything, it would seem.

"A white man at the Bible school is saying Liberia won't be at peace until Taylor is gone," our mission's detractors reported to the Taylor government's Ministry of Justice. Of course it wasn't true. No one would be stupid enough to say such a thing in a public setting. No one dared. But in a country where truth was of secondary importance to personal aggrandizement, the accusation was deadly serious.

With wild rumors of war swirling about, Liberian friends urged us to leave while we could. We knew Monrovia's relative peace could be shattered quickly and with no warning. In fact, several times we'd made a supply trip to town, only to find the stores' metal doors closed and barred. Store owners couldn't risk yet more loss of goods should rioting and looting begin, so when gunfire was heard on the edge of town they quickly closed up their shops.

IDP (Internally Displaced Persons) camp inside Liberia

It was April 2003 and time for our one-year home assignment anyway. Our hearts hurt for those who, unlike us, couldn't get away from the turmoil. The trapped included not only the tens of thousands of homeless Liberians who were on the run from recent attacks on their displacement camps, but also refugees from both the Ivory Coast's and Sierra Leone's wars. Unlike us, they didn't have the money to get on a plane and fly away. Unlike us, they had no friends and family in the U.S. to welcome them. Unlike us, they were completely trapped.

Chapter 19: The Upgrades

Within weeks of our leaving Africa, Taylor's military was fighting two separate rebel factions on the outskirts of Monrovia. It escalated and soon after that the "each man for himself" mentality that permeated the interior was, yet again, being played out in Liberia's beleaguered and over-crowded capital city. The rebels wanted Taylor out. They wanted the rubber, diamonds, gold, iron ore and timber for themselves. Demolishing Taylor and his government was the best way to make sure that happened. Mortars and rockets rained down on the city. Shell casings littered the streets.

People left their homes and sought shelter elsewhere, hoping there would be safety in numbers. Sixty thousand people flooded Monrovia's Samuel K. Doe Sports Stadium. No longer remotely safe and food increasingly scarce, they preferred the shelter of the bleachers to the insecurity of their homes. Others fled to schools and churches, some without any provisions. The most desperate slept in the streets. Staying alive became everyone's primary goal.

Liberians, horrified to be in the midst of yet another round of this senseless war and frustrated by the lack of international peacekeepers, piled seventeen dead bodies in front of a bullet-proof window at an entrance to the U.S. embassy compound. They demanded that journalists film the bodies. The world must see what was happening. The world must care about what was happening.

From the very beginning the Liberians had never been able to understand why the U.S. didn't stop their war. They considered themselves, because of the founding of their country by freed slaves, irrevocably tied to the United States. They were sure that if the U.S. President would just say the right words, things would change for the better. In fact, Taylor himself seemed to confirm that very idea. He stated to the Associated Press, "If one U.S. marine stood on Broad Street and blew a whistle, 'Time out,' then there would be peace." In the same interview he said, "When they arrive, Bingo... I would be out of here in a jiffy."[1]

And then finally, at long last, the U.S. did step in. President George W. Bush called Taylor on the telephone and told him he needed to leave Liberia.

Charles Taylor waves goodbye

On August 10, 2003, President Charles Taylor went on national T.V. and announced he was resigning and handing over the presidency to his vice president. And he did it—but not before complaining bitterly that his leaving Liberia would hurt the country.

The next day, with 2,300 U.S. Marines watching from three warships sitting off the coast, Taylor flew out of Liberia to exile in Nigeria. Upon his departure the Marines flew helicopters and Harrier jets from their ships to Monrovia, sending rebels fleeing into the bush. On the ground still other marines were welcomed as heroes. West African and then United Nations troops landed soon after and spread throughout Liberia, bringing

---

[1] http://ww2.aegis.org/news/lt/2003/lt030703.html accessed Jan.14, 2010.

The Upgrades

an enforced but welcome peace to a nation of shell-shocked people. With 200,000 dead and multiple thousands of its citizens dispersed to countries throughout the world, the population of Liberia was sorely depleted. But now, after fourteen years, the war was finally, at long last, really over.

The devastation in Liberia contrasted sharply with the peace and beauty of the Minnesota summer of 2003. We were deeply grateful to God for the timing and His provision for our departure and, of course, glad to be with family and friends. As we traveled to visit our financial and prayer supporters, people expressed gratitude for our faithfulness and treated us very kindly.

"I could never do what you do," they effused.

"You miss the point. *We* can't do what we do. It's God," we countered. They nodded at the obvious truth.

U.S. Marines in Monrovia

Mark's mother, a great friend and encourager, drove me to a ladies' meeting in rural Minnesota. "That was exhausting! It's not easy spilling your guts to a room full of strangers!" I said as I collapsed into the car's front seat afterward. She laughed. While Mark's mom was a very private, dry-eyed person, I teared up over a good Hallmark commercial. And I'd just emoted my way through my very personal and somewhat embarrassing testimony. I explained to my mother-in-law what was now clear to me; the way I thanked God for His amazing and ongoing work in my life was transparency with others. Perhaps they could learn from my surrenders. In fact, at this very event a young woman had jumped up and left the room crying as I listed what God had taken from me. She was in a time of great personal loss and recognized herself in my story. It had never occurred to her that God allowed it because He was trying to grow her. He would replace her losses with something much better. Himself.

It was our fourth one-year home assignment and we'd developed somewhat of a regular route as we visited supporting churches and individuals scattered throughout several States. This time as we traveled I noticed something different, but at first I couldn't put my finger on it. Then it hit me. Everyone had upgraded!

While young and just getting started in life, our friends and their children crowded into nice but somewhat confined living spaces. When we stayed overnight their children were put out of bedrooms to make room for us. Now as we traveled we were visiting the big, beautiful homes that had replaced the smaller, functional ones of earlier days. It was truly a pleasure to be in these houses, so what was my problem? Finally I figured it out; this niggling feeling at the back of my mind was jealousy.

What? I'm not the jealous type!

Or am I? I approached Mark, who was resting on a big, beautiful bed in a big, beautiful bedroom in yet another big, beautiful house. I poured out my confused thoughts. I was happy for my friends, but at the same time I was jealous. They were living in these beautiful houses while we were going back to yet another dilapidated mess. Yet that wasn't the thing that bothered me the most. The thing of which I was the most jealous was that my friend's lives all seemed so much easier than mine.

Mark listened without interruption. I spoke of the ongoing war in the Ivory Coast, the one just ending in Liberia, and the day-to-day realities of life in West Africa that an outsider would

The Upgrades

assume were the main problem. But these were not the things that burdened me the most. I was used to sickness, sores and the heat. Additionally, I knew if we wanted to live in West Africa we couldn't avoid the very real and negative results of their wars. The truth was that the problem that bothered me the most—the thing that made my life seem over-the-top difficult—was our detractors. Their accusations were so random and unpredictable that they created a constant threat to my serenity. Mark didn't argue my point and feeling better for having said it, I left the room.

An hour later I came back. Mark had been thinking about our situation and wanted to talk. "The problem with the church leaders is mine, not yours," he said, "and I don't expect you to bear my burden. However, I need a place where I can truly escape the pressure. I need you to create a haven for me."

Mark recognized that while God gave him grace to bear his load, I had grace for only what was rightfully my load. Not overconfiding was a way he could protect me. We made the decision that unless our detractors managed to get us deported from Liberia—something they'd tried very hard to do—and I needed to pack, Mark would keep me "out of the loop."

As for making a haven—now *that* was something I could do! In fact, I'd recently thought if I weren't a missionary I'd want to own and operate a Bed and Breakfast. I loved making things beautiful and homey. Because we were going to live about a mile inland from the ocean, I decided I wanted our house to have the feel of a seaside cottage. I could imagine the breeze blowing through soft, flowing curtains.

When we returned to Minneapolis after our long road trip, I began my create-a-haven project. I looked at paint color samples until I found the exact colors I wanted for various rooms. I bought the cloth I'd need for curtains. I chose summery dishes I loved. I bought a beautiful white table with six matching chairs from a local thrift store. No longer did I feel jealous of my friends; I didn't want their houses. I was creating our own seaside haven

Confessions of a Transformed Heart - Youth Edition

*Melodie, Nancy, Heidi, Mark,
John-Mark, Jared and Nathan—2003*

Chapter 20: Foolish Things

As we flew out of Minneapolis on June 16, 2004, our family was down from seven to five. John-Mark was preparing for his senior year and Melodie her sophomore year of college. Traveling with us were Nathan, who was seventeen, Heidi nine and Jared eight years old.

We stayed for two weeks in the Ivory Coast, saying good-bye to friends and packing a shipping container of our household goods to send to Monrovia. We were relieved that the worst of the tensions in that country seemed to be over and sincerely hoped the Ivorian people had learned from their Liberian neighbors the high cost of pursuing personal interest through war.

A small commuter plane took us from Abidjan to Monrovia. Not surprisingly, the city was in even worse condition than when we'd left it. Scars from the latest fighting were everywhere. Buildings were simply riddled with bullet holes and the infrastructure absolutely destroyed. Rainwater rushed through massive slums, home to tens of thousands of people who had fled the overwhelming instability in the country's interior. The vast majority of Liberia's approximately three million remaining citizens now lived in Monrovia—most in abject poverty.

Liberia now teemed with United Nations personnel. Their job, seemingly hopeless to the point of absurdity, was to create lasting peace through a show of force. Their mission was multifaceted, but the most obvious necessity for a lasting peace was getting the guns away from the thousands upon thousands of people who had participated in the war—some who wouldn't mind if it went on just a bit longer.

Liberia had changed as a result of the war. The rampant corruption, nepotism, tribalism, discrimination and exploitation that had so offended people when seen in their government leaders

Confessions of a Transformed Heart - Youth Edition

had moved down and was now apparent in every tier of the society. The pride and bellicose boldness normally reserved for someone with at least a modicum of power was now everywhere. Youth were disrespectful of their elders and many of the elders foolish and childish. After years of watching warlords use murder, terror and atrocities to get their own way—and often secretly or not-so-secretly admiring them for their successes—the moral fiber of the country was pathetically weak.

Guilt hung over the country like a thick, black cloud. This war should never have happened. Hundreds of missionaries had labored in Liberia, some for decades, bringing the message of the power of Christ to change lives. Tens of thousands of Liberians professed to be believers. With its Christian veneer—a mission, church, or ministry on almost every corner of Monrovia—a newcomer would assume nearly everyone must be a believer. But obviously this brand of Christianity lacked the power to produce any lasting change. Repentance of sin meant admitting you'd done it—although usually only if and when you were caught—not turning from it. And people didn't fear God enough to turn, much less flee, from even the most obvious sins. Their god was not holy, and everything, absolutely everything, was negotiable. 2 Timothy 3:5 seemed to explain it succinctly, "Having a form of godliness but denying the power thereof." Yet we knew even a nasty civil war would not cause God to negotiate His righteous standard. The war simply proved that what the Bible said in Isaiah 64:6 about everyone was true about the Liberians. "But we are all like an unclean thing, And all our righteousnesses are like filthy rags; We all fade as a leaf, And our iniquities, like the wind, Have taken us away."

Horrible as Liberia's spiritual condition was, and as impossible as it was for the U.N. to solve the problem with troops, guns and tanks, we knew it wasn't hopeless. True, these people were totally alienated from God by their sin. But also true, according to 2 Corinthians 5:18, it was for reconciliation Jesus had come. "Now all things are of God, who has reconciled us to Himself through Jesus Christ, and has given us the ministry of reconciliation."

As we made a home in Monrovia there were many changes for me. Most of them were good. After years in refugee work, primarily living in remote locations, I truly enjoyed living in a big city. While it was difficult to get used to the noise, confusion and uncertainties of a capital city just coming out of war, there were definite advantages. Not the least of these advantages was the easy access to the grocery stores—something I knew from personal experience should never be taken for granted!

I also enjoyed a very satisfying feeling of accomplishment. We'd not only survived refugee work, we had actually learned to thrive. We'd also persevered through the onslaught of our detractors and, to our great relief, they'd all officially separated from us and moved on. After years of trying to placate people to whom we were a continual disappointment, we were now working with Liberians who actually liked us personally and were appreciative of Baptist Mid-Missions' past and present work in Liberia. We were a much smaller, but happier group. With the war finally really over and our detractors officially gone, it felt like after more than fourteen years of living in a long and sometimes dark tunnel of uncertainty, we had crawled out into the glaring sunshine.

Several times a year we went into the interior of the country for Bible conferences and leadership seminars. With an excitement comparable to family week at a lively Christian camp, these people enjoyed fellowship and food. Most importantly, there was the opportunity for spiritual growth. I taught the women and Mark taught the men.

At a large conference of Liberian friends whom we'd come to love very much, one pastor to whom we were especially close introduced Mark as his "cousin," rather than the more traditional father. Unlike the role of a father, which made the missionary responsible for his children, the new relationship was one of camaraderie. We labored hand in hand and side by side with our "cousins" to bring the gospel to those who didn't know Christ.

And then, we worked together to train the new believers to be like Jesus.

Liberians now held positions of leadership that before the war had been filled by missionaries. Through their hardships and persecutions God had built an incredible strength into our friends that was truly a joy to behold. While we had no desire go backwards and recreate dependency, at the same time we could see that our role as missionaries was valuable. After years of working among them, many of our Liberian friends now trusted us enough to be totally blunt. Almost daily we were gaining a more clear understanding of the cultural values that had created the false gospel to which so many Liberians clung—a gospel that made a bloody fourteen-year civil war possible in a nation whose majority claimed to be Christians. We were uniquely qualified to "cut through the junk" and teach it straight!

Not surprisingly since the conflict had lasted fourteen years, Mark and I were the only ones left of the thirty adults on our original missionary team. It was we who had the privilege of working in this very changed and often overwhelmingly difficult Liberia.

Why had God chosen us? Why not someone else? Anyone else!

We suspected we knew. If God had used Mark in his original radio ministry people could have said, "Mark is so talented! Look what he's done!" But not now. Not with this. This ministry was something far removed from Mark's original gifts or talents. And while my ministry focus hadn't changed nearly as drastically as his, internally I was totally transformed. Both of us were. Through our trials God had prepared us to do a job we and everyone else knew could only be done through His strength. Perhaps God had chosen us because He knew if and when He used us, all glory would simply *have* to go to Him.

We had the dubious honor of being living examples of the truth of 1 Corinthians 1:27-29—"But God has chosen the foolish things of the world to put to shame the wise, and God has chosen the weak things of the world to put to shame the things which are mighty; and the base things of the world and the things which are despised God has chosen, and the things which are not, to bring to nothing the things that are, that no flesh should glory in His presence."

Chapter 21: Merri

While our daughter Melodie was in Liberia for three months in the summer of 2005 fulfilling the requirements of an internship for her college degree, she worked in an orphanage. She held Bible classes and clubs for the children, who ranged from toddlers to teens, and taught biblical principles for daily living, one-on-one, to several teenaged girls.

Melodie teaching at the orphanage

One afternoon Melodie flopped down beside me, a very serious look on her face. "I have something really important to talk about," she said in a shaky voice. My curiosity was piqued.

"There's a little girl at the orphanage with the look in her eyes of an animal just before it dies. Would it be O.K. if I brought her home and she stayed here for two weeks so we can figure out what's the matter with her?"

Through the years our children had rescued dozens of baby animals in a wide variety of health conditions. The eyes of those that didn't make it had a very distinctive look. If this child had that look, it was indeed serious. "I'll talk to Daddy about it," I said.

Mark agreed to the plan and a few days later the three of us went to the orphanage to pick up the little girl. Because Melodie worked primarily with the older children, she didn't know the name or anything else about the child we were hoping to take home with us. However, when we explained our mission to Jefferson, the orphanage's director, he immediately knew of whom we spoke and was grateful for our interest.

While waiting for someone to find her, Jefferson filled us in on the pitifully few details he had of her case. A year before the little girl had been found abandoned on the street and in deplorable condition. After a very brief stay at police headquarters, she'd been brought to the orphanage. Because she was mute, neither the police nor anyone else knew her name, her age or where she was from. The director chose Mary as her official name. It was the generic name given to nameless girls. Her nickname was a tribal word meaning bitterness. No one had ever seen her smile.

When I saw Mary my heart broke. She looked about the size of a three-year-old. Her eyes, one of which rolled lazily to the side, were glazed and swollen. Drool ran down her chin and onto the tattered baby t-shirt and shorts she wore. Mary's blotchy skin, sparse hair, worn adult teeth and deeply-furrowed eyebrows gave her a weird, elderly look.

Merri

Jefferson agreed to let Mary go home with us. She didn't resist when Melodie picked her up and placed her in the van. Nor did she seem concerned that we were leaving the orphanage and taking her with us. Too weak to manage the stairs, Melodie carried Mary to our second-story apartment. As they entered the living room everyone was silent—the silence that is natural in the presence of true suffering. Indeed, this tiny girl looked like all of the weight of the entire world rested on her skinny little shoulders.

We filled a plastic tub and as Mary stood in the warm water, fiercely scrubbing her scrawny limbs and distended tummy, we saw that her skin, with its grayish cast, was covered with sores.

The next day Melodie took Mary to a local clinic. The staff weighed and measured her: twenty-three pounds and thirty-six inches tall. Tests on her thin and weak-looking blood revealed an assortment of ailments including chronic malaria, anemia and an infection. She also had scabies all over her body and horrible sores lined her throat. Once home again, Mary pulled a four inch worm out of her mouth and gravely handed it to me.

We started her on a small pharmacy of medications that she fought with every ounce of her strength. At first we tried to gently coax her to cooperate, but after no success with that, we finally ended up forcing the medicine into her mouth and down her throat. Several times a day we repeated this process. Melodie and I would be sweating profusely by the time we finished. Mary had absolutely no sense that medication was given for her own good and we developed a real sympathy for the workers at the orphanage. With their more than one hundred children and only a few adults to care for them, fighting Mary about medicine probably hadn't seemed a priority.

Mary was extremely weak and couldn't do a lot of things, but the one thing she did very well was eat. And eat she did! With enthusiasm she ate the baby cereal we bought and with greater enthusiasm still she ate rice. Rice, rice and more rice. Three times a day she ate a huge bowl of rice topped with Liberian soup. She started to put on some much-needed weight.

But even more than for food, Mary was starved for affection. Each night when she began to look sleepy, I sat down on the sofa with her. Resting my cheek against her bony cheek, I scrunched down and held her tightly to me. She pushed in as closely as her body would allow. After about ten seconds she would pull back just enough to look me in the eye. I stared directly into her eyes, purposely radiating compassion. I wanted her to know I cared about the way she had suffered. She then pressed her face to my other cheek for about ten seconds. Then, again, she stared into my eyes. This went on for an hour or so until she fell asleep. Mary seemed desperate to know she was being looked at, being seen. How long had this child been invisible, alone in her own private world? I wondered.

And should we even call her Mary, the name for the nameless? Somehow it made her seem even more pathetic. Perhaps we could keep the name Mary but spell it M-E-R-R-I, trusting God to make her heart merry one day? That took a bit of faith. At this point I couldn't even imagine her face with a smile on it. Her eyes held the sadness of one who had seen too much of what little children shouldn't see, heard too much of what little children shouldn't hear, and knew more about life than anyone should know.

And so we started to think of her as Merri rather than Mary. To us it was significant; it meant hope. As I helped her get dressed I stared into her eyes, longing to see something other than the dead, flat look. As I held her in the evening when she fell asleep, I looked for even a flicker of a sparkle. Her deeply furrowed eyebrows seemed permanently etched in grief—hope something she probably couldn't remember feeling.

Several days after she arrived, Merri dipped a French fry in ketchup, took a bite and—a miracle—gave a slight smile. A few days after that our pet mongoose playfully nipped Melodie on the lip and, when everyone laughed, Merri gave a soft chuckle. And than eventually, at long last, something amused her and she grinned a grin that went all the way to her eyes. I felt like I'd been given the moon. It dawned on me—quite unexpectedly and suddenly—that I'd fallen in love with her.

"Maybe we should adopt her," I said to Mark, desperate to ensure her future safety and care. He pointed out that if we adopted Merri, her special needs could take us from our mission work in Liberia. While I could see his point was valid, I could also see the problem remained unsolved.

Then, in timing obviously of God, at a potluck dinner I met the very person I needed to help me with my dilemma. As Merri wandered from lap to lap and plate to plate, reveling in all the attention, my new friend and I talked—first about Merri and then about our lives, interests and ministries. As facts came out I realized that God Himself had orchestrated our meeting. This woman was the director of an international adoption agency, and most amazingly, it specialized in adoptions of special needs children. The more we talked the more my heart filled with hope. If it weren't actually happening I would've thought it too good to be true. Finally, unable to bear the suspense a moment longer, I begged shamelessly, "Do you think you could find a home for Merri?"

My new friend said that she thought she could do exactly that. She then asked me to write down some basic information about Merri on a piece of paper. Grabbing a scrap from my purse, I poise my pen. What should I write? I didn't know this little girl's name. No one did. So since it made no real difference, I spelled her name our new way, "M-e-r-r-i"—short for the longer, more official name I made up on the spot, Miracle Joy.

So the adventure continued, but now with the very real hope that Merri's future would be secure. Watching this child change before our eyes was truly fascinating and totally unlike anything our family had ever done before. Everyone was involved, pouring themselves into Merri and her needs. Each day we saw new signs of physical and emotional growth. Particularly notable was her attitude toward food. One day, after two weeks of eating like a starved man, Merri set aside a partially eaten bowl of rice and soup. She was full and didn't want any more. She appeared to understand there would always be food for her when she needed it, so no need to worry or to overeat. Merri's forehead, perpetually furrowed, at last began to relax.

We visited the orphanage again—this time to get permission to keep Merri in our home indefinitely. Merri was smiling and confident as she received her warm welcome from the staff and children. With a gain of nine pounds, skin clearing up from the scabies and increased strength as the infections disappeared, she was very noticeably changed.

Interestingly, Merri didn't seem the least afraid we'd leave her at the orphanage. She obviously considered herself a bona fide member of the Sheppard family. And why shouldn't she? We certainly treated her like a real family member. Throughout the day we touched her and held her. We gave her kisses and taught her to kiss us. It wasn't easy! Despite countless reminders—"Merri! Close your mouth when you give a kiss!"—she'd come at us with her mouth wide open and drool rolling down her chin. We smiled brightly as we mopped the drool from our faces. And as Merri relaxed into the love being offered her, she turned from a fearful, withdrawn child to a confident giver and receiver of love.

Very unexpectedly, caring for Merri lifted us up in the eyes of the Liberians. As first days, then weeks and finally months passed and Merri was still with us, still being treated as family, people couldn't help but take notice. Visitors in our home gasped audibly when she leaned in for a kiss, clearly dumbfounded we let her drool on our faces. When Merri screamed in frustration or anger and they witnessed firsthand that it wasn't an easy job we'd taken on, guests were forced to ask themselves why we bothered. People figured out it had to be love that motivated us because it was the only explanation that made any sense.

I remembered some years ago begging God to show me how to love. God had answered my desperate prayer and now used this little girl to show me how radically changed I was. This child had been a stranger to me only months before and, humanly speaking, had nothing to offer me. In fact, she was a tremendous amount of work, yet because she was mute couldn't even say the words, "Thank you." But I truly loved her. When she crawled into bed with me in the early hours of the morning and drooled her good morning kisses onto my face, I cried in wonder and amazement, "Who am I? Who have I become?"—knowing full well that this wasn't me; it was God in me.

Eight months after Melodie carried her up the stairs to our apartment, Merri walked down those same stairs for the last time. It was difficult to remember the weak, somber child of that first day. While she still drooled and she still couldn't talk, she could run and play. She had a huge smile that she showed us regularly. Merri was six inches taller and weighed nineteen pounds more than when she first came into our home. Her beautifully clear skin and thick black hair were the perfect coverings for her healthy interior.

Mark and Merri

Merri was on her way to North America and her new, adoptive family. They loved her, and no matter how little or how much Merri progressed under their care, they would continue to love her. She would be safe in their arms.

During the months Merri had been with us, God had used her to teach me a lot of things. Most notably, I realized that God was like these adoptive parents and I like Merri. Spiritually I was a poor, little girl cast out on the street and without hope, yet God had welcomed me into His family. He'd given me His name and invited me to share such intimacy with Him. In fact, according to Ephesians 1:3-6, God had adopted me.

> Blessed be the God and Father of our Lord Jesus Christ, who has blessed us with every spiritual blessing in the heavenly places in Christ, just as He chose us in Him before the foundation of the world, that we should be holy and without blame before Him in love, having predestined us to adoption as sons by Jesus Christ to Himself, according to the good pleasure of His will, to the praise of the glory of His grace, by which He has made us accepted in the Beloved.

These people were "redeeming" Merri from the streets of Monrovia, giving her their name and inviting her into their wonderful home not because Merri had something they lacked. No, it was because they were good and they'd chosen to love her. And similarly, it wasn't because I had something God needed that He'd adopted me, but because He was so good and He'd chosen to love me.

Several months after Merri was in her new home she was given a bone-density test, solving the mystery of her true age. Mary—twenty-three pounds, thirty-six inches tall when we brought her into our home—had been eleven years old. Upon hearing the information, I understood something very clearly. No matter what our future held, no matter what other opportunities God gave us, Merri would always be my family's finest work—our magnum opus.

Chapter 22: Grabbing Grace

We created the "seaside cottage" I'd envisioned on the second story of a large house our mission owned in Monrovia. It had formerly been a Bible Institute, but was now available to us. It was a massive project—the bullet holes in doors were some of the many reminders of the house's previous "tenants"—but eventually the whole building was useable. I'd never dreamed of having so much space at my disposal.

Foster babies Levi and Aerich

Five months into the time Merri was in our home, my friend with the adoption agency brought us a two-month old baby boy to foster. It'd been many years since our youngest was two months old and I'd all but forgotten what it was like caring for a baby twenty-four hours a day, seven days a week. Levi reminded me! And shortly following came another—one who was deathly ill. We experienced great joy as we watched Aerich turn from death to life. After this there were more. We had the privilege of fostering many babies and young children—some for days and some for many months—until they were able to go home to their new adoptive families.

Meanwhile my older children were leaving for college and beyond my reach. They had no home to go to during school breaks. They couldn't call us on the telephone and chat. We depended on friends, family and strangers to befriend them. We weren't disappointed. In gratitude to God for His provision for my children while they were in the United States, I took care of other people's young adult children who were visiting in Africa. Not only young people, but also hundreds of people of all ages passed through our home. On many nights more than twenty people slept under our roof. Countless more sat at our table. We hosted diplomats, pastors, missionaries, United Nations personnel and adoptive parents. Nationalities included Americans, Belgians, Canadians, Lebanese, Irish, Germans and, of course, Liberians.

On top of my homemaking and hospitality responsibilities, my foster care work, teaching ministry and correspondence, I was home-schooling Heidi and Jared. I loved every ministry in which I was involved, but things had come one at a time until I felt like the proverbial frog sitting in the pot of gradually heating water. I was working like crazy all day and then up with babies several times in the night. Every dream of mine had come true—helping my husband, caring for orphans, a Bed and Breakfast (such as it was), teaching women and home-schooling my children—but, unfortunately, all my dreams had come true at the same time!

One Sunday afternoon I flopped down in exhaustion as a vanload of guests headed to the airport. On its return it was bringing new guests. Supposedly this was my "day of rest," but how could I rest when all I could think about were dirty sheets and towels needing to be changed and floors needing to be swept? It was too much!

Grabbing Grace

"God, you say in your Word You won't give us more than we can bear, [1]but this is perilously close," I sobbed.

Needing sympathy, I e-mailed Karen. She was always good for sympathy. But even as I wrote the letter explaining my predicament, I couldn't see anything I was willing to drop. It seemed each door of ministry was one God had opened for me. Nevertheless, I hoped there was a solution.

My sister wrote back the next day, sympathetic and sweet. She couldn't figure out how anyone juggled my load. No one runs a Bed and Breakfast at the same time they do foster care, she pointed out. But she also could see each ministry was of God. Karen didn't feel the answer was to drop things. God would give the grace necessary.

That was it. I didn't need less work; I needed more grace. Even before Karen's response arrived, I'd reached the same conclusion. Each task was important. Each was something I knew God was asking me to do at this season of my life. I must grab the grace God offered for each moment and hang on to it—not panic about tomorrow with its possible sleep deprivation or work overload. His grace was sufficient for me and to be claimed moment by moment, not in advance.

Within a couple of days a Liberian friend rushed into the house. "The people with the electric are just down the streets!" he announced excitedly.

"See if you can get them here!" I said quickly. My hopes were soaring.

After more than fourteen years without city electricity, our section of Monrovia was the first to be electrified. The first time I flipped a switch and a light went on—no loud beating of a generator in the background—it felt like a miracle. Heidi and Jared could do more schoolwork on the computer. I could use a crockpot. I could wash clothes without raising and lowering the hose three times each load. In a hundred different ways, some large and some small, city electricity simplified my life.

---

[1] 1Corinthians 12:9

God taught my entire family more of biblical servanthood through this intensely busy time in our lives and, thankfully, gradually my responsibilities lessened. But I had the joy of knowing I'd persevered. When it was more than I could bear, God gave more grace. And some of the grace poured through electrical wires.

Chapter 23: Mouse Poison

"Do you know where the mouse poison is?" Mark asked one Sunday morning.

"I don't know anything about that," I stated hurriedly.

I was flying through the room trying to do six things at once. In contrast Mark was seated cross-legged on the bed, looking far too relaxed to please me and far from being able to give me a hand. My life was incredibly busy on a normal day, and this wasn't a normal day. With a picnic to prepare, besides getting the family and foster babies off to church, I didn't have time to worry about mouse poison.

"I don't like it when you say, "I don't know anything about that," Mark said pointedly.

What? Is this a *joke?* I thought irritably.

I said aloud. "What's wrong with saying, 'I don't know anything about that'?"

"It feels like you're not taking what I'm asking seriously," Mark answered.

I wasn't pleased. After all, how seriously do I *need* to take a question about mouse poison on a Sunday morning? I shared my less-than-happy thoughts with Mark and, before I knew it, we were embroiled in a stupid and absolutely pointless argument. So throwing out every lesson I not only knew but also taught at well-attended ladies' seminars, I decided to punish Mark with stone cold silence.

With incredible acting skill I interacted with people at church. I attended the picnic and came back home again, all without directing one word at Mark. By nightfall he was thoroughly tired of being ignored and confronted me about the silent treatment he'd been receiving. It didn't go well for either of us.

Mark was more than a bit irritated. In an ongoing defense of his original question, he reiterated that he didn't like it at all when I said, "I don't know anything about that." He found it dismissive. And besides, he suspected it wasn't entirely true—that, indeed, I *did* know something about the mouse poison.

"Well, I'm irritated too," I said. "I don't mind you confronting me when I'm sinning, but this is too much. It isn't a sin to say, 'I don't know anything about that,' so quit *tweaking* me!" The sun didn't set on our wrath (Ephesians 4:26), but it didn't set on our complete bliss either. Not by a long shot.

The real issue wasn't mouse poison, of course. The problem was that, having invested ourselves in the argument, neither of us was willing to concede. It wasn't the first time in our marriage this had happened.

"Dear God, please show me the answer," I prayed. "I need Your wisdom. If we come to a wall in our relationship—something neither of us can figure out how to get through—what should we do? If we, the teachers, don't have the answers, who does?"

About two weeks before this "discussion" I was reading *Creative Counterpart* by Linda Dillow. She took her readers to Philippians 2:5-8.

> Let this mind be in you which was also in Christ Jesus, who, being in the form of God, did not consider it robbery to be equal with God, but made Himself of no reputation, taking the form of a bondservant, and coming in the likeness of men. And being found in appearance as a man, He humbled Himself and became obedient to the point of death, even the death of the cross.

At the time I read it I didn't think too much about those verses. Because they were familiar I assumed I already understood what they were saying. However, several days after our tiff Mark and I were on our way to the grocery store, and as we bumped over potholes and wove our way through the busy afternoon traffic, those verses pulsed in my head. I knew God was telling me something. The answer to Sunday's problem was somewhere in those verses. But what was God saying?

Mouse Poisen

He humbled Himself and became obedient to the point of death, even the death of the cross.

Jesus *humbled* Himself. That was it! The contrast between His behavior and mine was marked. He died naked on the cross, voluntarily humbling Himself before His enemies. I couldn't bear being misunderstood about mouse poison in front of my husband.

My pride had created the impasse with Mark. Although his timing was poor, it hadn't been sin for Mark to ask me where the mouse poison was. The real problem started when I got defensive and then angry when he wasn't satisfied with my quick response. It hurt my pride. And the answer was humility. I knew that. But it was one thing to know it and another to really practice it. However, if I didn't want more mouse poison incidents, I had to choose to be like Jesus, Who humbled Himself even to the point of death.

So, parked in front of the grocery store with an assortment of disabled beggars looking on, I asked Mark to forgive me. "I understand now," I said. "When we come to a wall in our relationship—something too difficult to go through—God is telling me I must be humble and go *under* the wall. I must be like Jesus."

Several weeks later I found the mouse poison. It was just where I had put it.

Chapter 24: Preston

We met Preston in 1993 when this handsome, gregarious man was but a young teen. In the years since he'd worked with various missionaries, including us. He'd been active in the churches in which we'd ministered and even gone to Bible school in the Ivory Coast for several semesters.

In 1999 Preston married Tasha, a very beautiful and quiet young woman from the church we helped start in Bloléquin. We were happy he found such a sweet young lady. She was even a virgin, a rare find indeed.

When we returned to Liberia in 2004 after our one-year home assignment, we heard Preston was living in Monrovia. Mark was able to contact him and invite him over to talk. Because the city was full of thieves who took advantage of the black nights and our vacant house with only its low cement wall around it for protection was an obvious target, we needed an honest watchman to guard it while we were renovating. Preston was a logical choice.

On one of Preston's first nights working his new job, a group of seven thieves quietly jumped the wall. They grabbed things from the clothesline and yard. Preston, hearing the rustle of grass and soft movement of feet, called loudly for help. This roused a neighbor man and together they chased the surprised thieves from the yard.

We appreciated Preston's courage and obvious loyalty. When we moved into the house we asked Preston and Tasha, along with their two little daughters, to live downstairs. In exchange for rent, he was responsible for answering any knocks at the gate in the evening and making sure the night watchmen we hired were doing their jobs. Mark offered him a day job helping around the house and yard. We loaned Preston money so he could set up a little teashop right outside our yard to bring in extra cash. So his

Bible school education could continue, Mark helped pay his tuition.

One night, more than two years later, our son John-Mark walked into our yard and interrupted a huge fight. Preston's hand was on Tasha's throat and he was bellowing at his pastor, also present, accusing him of aiding Tasha in prostitution. Tasha's face was bruised and her neck was streaked where the skin had been peeled away by Preston's fingernails. We were horrified.

We knew before we invited them to live downstairs from us that their marriage had problems, but we had no idea it was that bad. Foolishly we assumed that the counseling Preston had previously received, his Bible school education (he'd just passed the Christian Home course Mark taught), and his years in church had matured him. Obviously we were wrong. We insisted Preston and Tasha accept counsel for their deeply troubled marriage. Preston, chagrined he'd been caught so royally, cooperated fully.

We found the sessions truly enlightening as Tasha filled us in on what had been going on behind the scenes—most of it since the very beginning of their marriage. Preston was a very jealous husband and everything, no matter how insignificant, was a sign of Tasha's infidelity. If she arrived home from the market a few minutes late, she was seeing a lover. If she came home in a taxi from the wrong direction, obviously she was committing adultery. When he followed her to the market and she stepped out of his line of vision, she was meeting up with a boyfriend. Not surprisingly, Tasha was deeply angry about the false accusations and the abuse.

We gave them advice from the Bible and prayed with them. We hoped it would help, and maybe it did in the short-term. But six months later the problem was back. This time there was a new twist. With no credible evidence, Preston was accusing a trusted pastor, a personal friend of ours, of being involved with his wife. It was simply preposterous, but, nevertheless, had the potential to destroy our friend's Christian testimony. At that point, totally fed up, Mark told Preston that if he beat his wife again or accused anyone else of adultery with her, he'd lose his job, be evicted from our house, and be put out of the Bible school.

Things quieted down for a while. However, several months after the ultimatum, Tasha appeared on our porch. Skin was raked off her neck and there were two large bruises on her face. "I am so tired," she whispered. "I am so tired."

After Mark called their pastor and a Bible school authority as witnesses, he confronted Preston for his wicked behavior and reiterated the consequences. He then turned to Tasha and asked her what she planned to do. Hunched over and weeping profusely, Tasha whispered that she wanted to separate from Preston. Clearly she felt her situation was hopeless.

After Tasha finished, Preston spoke up boldly. He defended his abuse of Tasha and said he was finished with her. He was obviously furious with Tasha not only for her "adultery," but also for telling us about the accusations and the latest beating.

Then after he had said his piece, very unexpectedly and to everyone's complete horror, Preston jumped up, grabbed each of his little daughters by a hand and marched them off the yard. No one had the slightest idea where he was taking them.

It was the perfect revenge and he knew it. That night we could hear Tasha's agonized wailing from her downstairs room. When I brought her a plate of food, I found her clutching her daughters' clothing and crying, "My little girls! My little girls!"

The next day Preston was back. In typical Liberian fashion he had brought a proxy to "talk the case" for him. As he sat to the side, head bowed humbly, his sister made her emotional appeal on his behalf. With tears streaming down her face she told us Preston was sorry for beating Tasha. He would never do it again. Please let him keep his job. Her pleas were impassioned and heartfelt. Could we please reconsider? Think of Tasha and the girls! If Preston lost his job and was evicted, what would happen to them?

We didn't doubt for a minute Preston's entire extended family was sorry he had beaten his wife yet again and was equally sorry he was losing his job over it. Unfortunately, their sorrow didn't erase Preston's sinful behavior nor take away its consequences. When he saw his sister's pleas weren't going to win back his position, Preston dropped the contrite look.

We moved to the next subject, which was Tasha's plan for her future. Because of Preston's dangerous desire to take the girls from her, she was in an awful position. If she refused to go back to him, Preston had already proven that he would indeed take them. If she stayed with him she could be with her daughters who very desperately needed her, but she would continue to be in danger. Now as she sat on the sofa pouring tears and looking positively wretched after her sleepless night, she quietly announced her decision. She would stay with Preston.

Tasha had the right to make that decision. Since we did not wish to make things more difficult for her than they already were, we said that she and the girls could stay in their downstairs room until Preston found another place for the family to live.

When the meeting ended, Mark calculated Preston's legal severance pay. Although it was galling that after all we'd given him we had to give more to get rid of him, we didn't want trouble. Besides, we knew we were doing the right thing by letting him go—whatever the cost. Perhaps if Preston were forced to suffer the consequences of his sin, he just might decide his jealousy wasn't worth it.

Three weeks later a battered pickup pulled into the yard. Preston hopped out and began quickly loading their possessions, eyes averted from us. When at last he was finished we hugged Tasha and the little girls good-bye, pressing gifts into their hands. Our hearts hurt. They'd lived in our house for almost two years and it felt like we were saying good-bye to a beloved daughter and precious grandchildren.

After the pickup with its bulging load rolled out of the yard, I went into action. There was no time to stand around mourning. We'd invited a young lady to live with us for a couple of months and I needed to get the room cleaned up so it could be repainted. I called Jared to help me. As we entered the vacated room I saw a ripped calendar falling off the wall, a couple of empty Coke bottles, some empty mayonnaise jars and, in the center of the room, a large box of what looked like discarded papers. I flipped through the old notebooks, class notes and loose papers to see if anything looked valuable. It didn't. Tearing the calendar off the wall and adding it to the box, I sent Jared outside to burn it. After a few more minutes I joined him and together we watched the papers go up in flames.

Two weeks later, Preston showed up, angry and determined. We'd burned $100,000, he claimed. It'd been in the box. He threatened legal action against us if we didn't give him the money.

It was sheer craziness. One hundred thousand Liberian dollars was the equivalent of about $1,600 United States dollars. Where in the world would Preston get so much money? And assuming he had it, wouldn't it be foolishness itself to leave it behind in the center of an unlocked room? There was no way there was money in that box. That many Liberian dollars would've filled the entire box and I'd flipped through the whole thing. And then, most importantly and absolutely irrefutably, Jared and I had watched the whole box of papers burn and we saw not one bill, much less $100,000 worth.

But, nevertheless, the accusation stood and I was completely stunned. What was he *doing?* We'd loved Preston, Tasha and their little daughters as if they were family. We gave Preston a job. We let his family live in our house. We bought them Christmas presents. We played with the little girls. We gave and gave and gave. And this was his way of saying thank you? I felt betrayed.

Mark and our pastor friends begged Preston to stop this madness, but Preston wouldn't listen to any voice of reason. Then, several days later, we received a summons. Mark and I were to go to the Temple of Justice to discuss with the city attorney some accusations concerning destruction of personal property. Friends informed us that there was no such thing as a simple meeting at the Temple of Justice and they suggested we bring a lawyer to the consultation. We e-mailed our supporters in the U.S., asking for special prayer. Mark was afraid this would turn into years of defending himself in court. We knew from bitter experience it was a very real possibility.

The day of the consultation arrived. Never before had I been called in on such a case. But since I was the one who had asked Jared to burn the box of papers, there was no question I was involved.

I needed God's guidance. How should I handle this? With only an hour before our departure for the four o'clock meeting, I reached for my Bible. I noticed a nearby book leaning over a bit and pulled it off the shelf. It was a book of Puritan prayers entitled *Valley of Vision*. I flipped it open. The friend who had given it to me had filled in the special presentation page with a sweet note, the date and the scripture reference, Philippians 2:5-11.

Hey, I knew those verses! They were the "mouse poison" verses! Scrambling for my Bible I found the familiar passage and read it through several times. Each spoke clearly, but especially notable were verses five to eight.

> Let this mind be in you which was also in Christ Jesus, who, being in the form of God, did not consider it robbery to be equal with God, but made Himself of no reputation, taking the form of a bondservant, and coming in the likeness of men. And being found in appearance as a man, He humbled Himself and became obedient to the point of death, even the death of the cross.

Then I read from the book my friend had given me. I was amazed. It was as though this Puritan had written this prayer for me alone and for this very day.

<u>The Valley of Vision</u>
Lord, High and Holy, Meek and Lowly,
Thou hast brought me to the valley of vision,
Where I live in the depths but see Thee in the heights;
Hemmed in by mountains of sin I behold Thy glory.

Let me learn by paradox
That the way down is the way up,
That to be low is to be high,
That the broken heart is the healed heart,

That the contrite spirit is the rejoicing spirit,
That the repenting soul is the victorious soul,
That to have nothing is to possess all,
That to bear the cross is to wear the crown,
That to give is to receive,
That the valley is the place of vision.

Lord, in the daytime stars can be seen from deepest wells,
And the deeper the wells the brighter thy stars shine;
Let me find Thy light in my darkness,
Thy life in my death,
Thy joy in my sorrow,
Thy grace in my sin,
Thy riches in my poverty,
Thy glory in my valley. [1]

I grabbed a 3x5 card. "The way down is the way up. To be low is to be high," I scrawled quickly. I wrote out several of the verses from Philippians. This was my answer. The way to handle this betrayal with the right attitude was to handle it just like Jesus handled His betrayal. I must be like Jesus.

My stomach knotted as we drove the five miles to the Ministry of Justice building in central Monrovia. I fingered the 3x5 card, glancing periodically at the words, my "crib notes."

Preston was waiting in the hall outside the assigned room, and when I saw him I was shocked. In place of the handsome young man I knew was a hollow-eyed skeleton. His eyes were red-rimmed and scary-looking. He looked totally hardened.

"Hello, my son," I greeted him. I must be like Jesus.

"What are the white people doing here?" I heard someone ask as we waited.

"Destruction of property." How embarrassing.

We, along with the pastor friends who had accompanied us, were invited into the room with Preston and his delegation. The

---

[1] Edited by Arthur Bennett, *The Valley of Vision*, Carlisle, PA, The Banner of Truth Trust, 2005, 24-25.

city attorney sat at a desk in the front of the room with chairs pulled in a semicircle around it. Two chairs were put directly in front of the desk for Mark and me.

The attorney introduced himself and immediately got to the point. This was a case about the destruction of personal property, he said. Nancy Sheppard had destroyed Preston's property and it was a crime.

A *crime?* And I alone was being accused—not Mark and me? Forgetting the 3x5 card and the fact Jesus was silent before His accusers, I placed my hand on the desk. The attorney glanced at me, giving me permission to speak.

"*Surely* it's not a crime to burn garbage in Liberia," I said.

He answered harshly, "Destruction of personal property is a criminal offense!"

"I'm being called a *criminal!*" I cried out in horror to no one in particular. It felt like a blow straight to the face.

Four pastors jumped out of their chairs and simultaneously patted my back. "They called Jesus a criminal too," one reminded, patting furiously.

Horrified and humiliated by what was happening, I moved to the far corner of the room, trying to get out of view. I sobbed and sobbed; I couldn't stop. I pawed through my purse for a Kleenex but found none. Hot tears dripped down my face, soaking my skirt. Everyone politely ignored me, in the corner of the room awash with tears.

A mutual friend interrupted the proceedings. Standing before the entire group, he begged Preston to reconsider. Did we have to go on? Couldn't this matter be settled by a group of pastors in a private setting? Must it be in the courts? Preston, perhaps shamed by my tears, conceded. Mark eagerly agreed to settle it elsewhere. The meeting was brought to a close and people left the room.

As I shakily stood up, I noticed that only a few people remained. One of them was Preston. It dawned on me that God was giving me the opportunity to obey Him and to do what He had told me to do—to be like Jesus.

Feeling like this was somehow happening outside of myself, its importance very clear, I fell on my knees before Preston. With tears still streaming down my face, I told Preston that I wished I could wash his feet. Right before His betrayal Jesus had washed Judas' feet, and I wanted to be like Jesus. Reaching up from my kneeling position, I grabbed Preston around his neck and hugged him tightly. "I love you," I said. "And if you kill me I will love you even while the knife is twisting into me." I then kissed him on the cheek.

Preston was exquisitely uncomfortable. He squirmed against the wall, trying to escape my embrace. "Listen to the lady!" his lawyer demanded, pushing him down into his chair. At the same time the city attorney, embarrassed that the white lady was on her knees, was pulling on my shoulder, trying to drag me to my feet.

"No, I must be like Jesus. I must love Preston," I explained earnestly, looking up at the attorney. "Even though he betrayed me, I must still love him. We haven't loved Preston perfectly, but we've loved him our best."

As we left the Ministry of Justice building and headed back home, my heart was at complete peace. I had no control over the outcome, but I was content that I had done what God asked me to do.

A group of pastors met with Preston and Mark to discuss the case. Not one would back Preston in even one of his accusations. Shamed, Preston disappeared from our lives and we heard nothing from him and little about him.

More than a year later Preston phoned to ask if he could come to the house to speak with us. He wanted the pastor whom he'd accused of an improper relationship with Tasha to be there also. We agreed to the meeting.

Preston came, bringing his new pastor and Tasha with him. After nervous greetings and uncomfortable small talk, he opened up. He told of a series of horrible and humbling events in his life. His sins that had taken him from his job, his friends and his school had, not surprisingly, eventually completely torn apart his marriage. However, after seven months of separation, He and

Tasha were together again. Their pastor was presently counseling them.

Preston apologized to Mark and me for his behavior. He also asked forgiveness of the pastor whom he'd wrongfully accused. He appeared sincere. Tasha, at his side, looked relaxed and happy. She assured me he was behaving appropriately. I was pleased to witness God's ongoing work in their lives.

I was also pleased God had used this trial to continue His purifying work in my life. During the time between the event at the Ministry of Justice building and the apology, I'd come to understand that even if Preston never did admit fault, even if he never asked forgiveness, this trial had value. I was learning how to identify with Jesus, and in the process becoming more like Him. The words of a beautiful old hymn were my prayer:

> Oh! to be Like Thee
> Oh! to be like Thee, blessed Redeemer.
> This is my constant longing and prayer;
> Gladly I'll forfeit all of earth's treasures
> Jesus, Thy perfect likeness to wear.
>
> Oh! to be like Thee, full of compassion,
> Loving, forgiving, tender and kind,
> Helping the helpless, cheering the fainting,
> Seeking the wand'ring sinner to find.
>
> Oh! to be like Thee, lowly in spirit,
> Holy and harmless, patient and brave;
> Meekly enduring cruel reproaches,
> Willing to suffer, others to save.
>
> Oh! to be like Thee, while I am pleading,
> Pour out Thy Spirit, fill with Thy love,
> Make me a temple meet for Thy dwelling,
> Fit me for life and Heaven above.
>
> *Refrain:*
> Oh! to be like Thee. Oh! to be like Thee.
> Blessed Redeemer, pure as Thou art;

Preston

Come in thy sweetness, come in thy fullness.
Stamp Thine own image deep on my heart.[2]

---

[2] Thomas O. Chisholm, O*h! to be Like Thee*, published 1897, Public Domain.

Epilogue

On our fifth one-year home assignment God gave us a wonderful surprise—a week in Orlando, Florida. Melodie came from Indiana where she was attending a biblical counseling training course. Nathan was on his spring break from college. Unbelievably, John-Mark came on a two week, transportation-paid vacation from his Liberian ministry. Our family of seven was together in vacation paradise.

And then to make Mark especially happy about the whole thing, my father and stepmother paid for our stay at a great timeshare condo. It was part of a beautiful resort—complete with mini-golf, paddleboats, thirteen swimming pools and hot tubs. They also took us to the Arabian Knights dinner theater. As if all of this weren't enough, members of a supporting church gave us six one-day "Park Hopper" tickets to the four Disney theme parks.

Park Hopper Day rose clear and warm. By its nine o'clock opening time we were in front of the Animal Kingdom, feeling quite at home in our lush, tropical surroundings. We were ready to seriously "hop." Because it was off-season the lines for the attractions weren't too long, so despite our time constraint—one-day tickets—we felt confident we could visit all the parks.

The gates opened and we hit the ground running. After several fun yet relatively tame rides, we arrived at "Expedition Everest." The advertising boasted, "Take on the treacherous terrain of the towering Forbidden Mountain in this high-altitude, high-speed train adventure. Nail-biting hairpin turns hurl you forward toward the peak and then, just when you think it couldn't get more thrilling—backward! The mountain's full of surprises: Beware the snarling beast who watches over his domain... the Yeti."

Our family held its private secret as we screamed and laughed on Expedition Everest; we had ridden the *real* expedition. We took on the treacherous terrain of the unknown, forbidden mountains of fear and doubt, the high-speed adventure of trust in God. We did go backwards at times and the mountain certainly was full of surprises. The snarling beast was definitely watching over his domain. The hairpin turns of our own expedition hurled us forward toward the peak.

I was aware of the grandeur of the mountain peak as Mark and I walked in the mass of sun-baked humanity with our five beautiful children. John-Mark, twenty-five years old, was now a missionary, sharing the gospel with Muslims in West Africa. He was a man, strong and godly. Melodie at twenty-three was beautiful inside and out. Her heart was soft and she dearly loved "the least of these," the orphans of Africa. Nathan, twenty-one years old, with his outgoing, "never-met-a-stranger" personality amazed me. He was a billboard of everything a college-aged young man should be. Heidi, thirteen, was growing more physically and spiritually lovely each day. Jared, at twelve, was a ball of sunshine and joy.

Epilogue

We "hopped" to Disney's Magic Kingdom. Cinderella's castle was a perfect backdrop for a photo shoot. Heidi snapped pictures of Melodie, Jared and Mark skipping playfully, smiling rapturously like models for a brochure. Then Mark took pictures of the five kids lined up in a row, jumping together. By this time we had an audience. People saw the silliness and smiled along with us. Our children all looked so much alike there was no doubting they were siblings. I felt we should be the envy of everyone.

With organizational skills honed by twenty-two years of international travel, we maneuvered Disney's Animal Kingdom, the Magic Kingdom and Hollywood Studios. By nine o'clock in the evening all the parks were winding down and we were at Epcot Center, the last of the four parks. Our feet were dead tired and we were about "hopped" out, but good stewardship of the Park Hopper tickets demanded we hop 'til we drop—or until they locked us out of the park.

The Soarin' ride looked exciting. It promised the "rush of a lifetime to hang glide over the Golden Gate Bridge and California's Redwood forest." After waiting in line with hundreds of sunburned tourists, we were locked into our seats, seven Sheppards in a row.

It was thrilling indeed. We responded in unison to the stomach-tumbling adventure of soarin' over mountains and lakes and forests. We held up our fourteen tired feet when a crash appeared imminent. We delighted in the wondrous beauty—together.

As we stumbled our way off the ride and into the light I noticed Mark was quiet. Holding me to himself he said with tear-filled eyes, "We have the best family. Look at them. They love each other." The children noticed our clinch and joined us for a group hug.

The opportunity to participate in something of true value changes children just like it changes adults. Mark's and my struggles through the years have been huge and we've discussed often and at length the right way to handle them, many times including the children in these discussions. We couldn't protect them from life, but by God's grace we could give them the tools to handle it. "You've given us the best gift of all," Melodie had said recently. "You taught us to think biblically."

Luke 14:26 is a weird, difficult to understand, verse. It says,

> If anyone comes to Me and does not hate his father and mother, wife and children, brothers and sisters, yes, and his own life also, he cannot be My disciple.

At first glance it looks like Jesus is teaching hate. But of course Jesus isn't telling us to *hate* our children. Rather He's saying that in comparison to our love for Christ, our love for our children will look like hate. It's a biblical paradox: when we choose God we're choosing what's best for us. As a corollary to this, when we choose God we're also choosing what's best for our children.

I remember with sadness those two young wives who kept their husbands from missionary work because they felt it not best for their children. Oh, what those children missed!

It's true that our children haven't gone to the "best schools." There have been times their haircuts were atrocious and their clothes ripped and stained. They've suffered malaria, trichinosis, schistosomiasis, typhoid, scabies, dysentery and infected sores galore. We missed both John-Mark's and Melodie's college graduations and will doubtless miss countless more special occasions in the future.

But what have they gained? Everything they needed and then some. They certainly had very interesting childhoods. Besides the variety of experiences and opportunities that work among war refugees afforded my children, there were other less obvious, yet very real, advantages. They could speak Liberian English like real Liberians and they could speak conversational French. They knew music, stories and jokes from around the world. They had dined with diplomats and ambassadors. As well as living in Liberia and the Ivory Coast, one or all of them had visited France, England, Switzerland, Holland, Belgium, Spain, Lebanon, Korea, Ireland, Mexico, Guinea, Mali and Sierra Leone. They *believed* the rest of the world existed; they'd been there.

Epilogue

And what have I gained? Everything I ever wanted.

Years ago in Bloléquin as baby Jared's health declined and we prayed like we'd never prayed for anything in our lives, Mark said, "Every term God has taught us something new. Maybe this term He's going to teach us how to pray." I hardly dared believe it could be true, but God did teach me just that.

Our first term in Liberia, I served. It was wonderful, but even as I saw God give fruit for my service I cried, "It isn't enough. It's never enough." God wanted something so much more than my idol of Christian service. Our second term, now in refugee work, God taught me submission—both to Mark and to God. And to my surprise, rather than stifling me, this perceived loss of control actually freed me. Our third term, despite my doubts, God taught me to pray. The fourth term God taught me to reverence Mark, which not only honored him, but even more importantly also showed honor for God and His Word. And in our fifth term God taught me what Christ-like humility looked like.

"This is not the woman I married," Mark said to a friend. Startled, she glanced at me, making sure I was O.K. with what Mark had just said. Yes, I was O.K. with it. I knew it was true. Very basic parts of my personality were changed as my "idols" were toppled.

Idols? Yes. Not wooden or stone idols, of course, but things on which I set my heart (Ezekiel 14:1-5). Lou Priolo says it well. "An idol can be anything. It may even be a good thing. But if we want it so badly that we sin if we don't get it or sin to attain it, then we're worshipping an idol rather than Christ."[1]

God knew me so much better than I knew myself and loved me too much to leave me as I was. He wanted all of my worship, so He tore down my idols. He used the unique circumstances in which He'd placed me—circumstances I initially resented—to put to death the "Old Nancy" so He could resurrect a "New Nancy."

---

[1] Lou Priolo, Class notes on "Idols of the Heart," (Atlanta Biblical Counseling Center), 1994, quoted in Martha Peace, *The Excellent Wife: A Biblical Perspective*, Bemidji, MN, Focus Publishing, 1999, p.59.

God didn't reject me for my sin—to much of which I'd been oblivious. Instead He lavished His grace and mercy on me by first showing me my sin and then showing me how to change. God's Spirit made God's Book come alive to me and then provided the power I needed to obey it.

Am I radically transformed? Absolutely. Am I perfect? Absolutely not. Do I have all the answers? No. But this I do know. Because I didn't have an unflinching trust in God, I floundered when I couldn't figure out what He was doing. I begged God to show me who He really was and He answered that prayer. When I yielded control of my life to God, He became not only my lord and master, but also my friend and brother. My beloved. And it was enough.

Appendix 1: Intercessory Prayer Requests for Liberia

1. I pray that God would provide daily food, clothing and shelter for the Liberian people.
2. May God open up the hearts and minds of the Liberians to understand God's message of salvation; may He make blind eyes see.
3. I ask God to make a way for the unreached counties, towns and villages of Liberia to hear of the salvation He offers.
4. I pray that God would bring down corrupt religious leaders and those spreading a false gospel.
5. May Jesus continue to reveal Himself to the Muslims of Liberia as the only way to heaven.
6. I ask that the Liberians would see the futility of life without Christ.
7. May the Liberians be freed from their fear of evil spirits.
8. I ask that God would show his power to be greater than the power of the zoes (spirit communicators) and molimen (Islamic shamen).
9. May the believers repent of their sin and live in a way honoring to their Lord and Savior.
10. May God make the Christian men of Liberia to be true men of God—servant-leaders in their homes, churches and work places.
11. I pray that the Christian women of Liberia would repent of their rebellion against their husbands.
12. May God cause the hearts of the children to be turned to the heavenly Father.
13. I ask that God would raise up Christian leaders with a real heart for the youth of Liberia.
14. May God revive the hearts of the Liberian believers and make the truths of His Word real to them.
15. I pray that God would fill believers with the peace and joy promised in His Word.

16. I ask that God would raise up Godly leaders who will teach others.
17. I pray Mark and Nancy Sheppard would be blessed with wisdom to know which ministries to pursue and how to pursue them.
18. I pray God would raise up a generation of Liberians who are committed to fulfilling the Great Commission in their own country and beyond.
19. I pray God would raise up intercessors for the people of Liberia.
20. May the name of our Lord and Savior Jesus Christ be made great in Liberia!

Appendix 2: How to be Changed from the Inside Out

The following excerpt is from *The Excellent Wife*. The passage has been modified to be more appropriate for youth. It is used with the permission of its author Martha Peace and was adapted from material developed by Stuart Scott.[1]

Believers have a God-given capacity to have a pure devotion to and worship of the Lord Jesus Christ, but they frequently struggle with other "gods"/lusts/cravings competing for their affections. These "desires" are not necessarily bad. For example, going fishing is fun and certainly not sinful. However, idolatry comes into play at the point that the fisherman does not get to go on a planned trip and he sins. The problem is his affections are set on fishing, not on the Lord Jesus. Fishing could possibly have become an idol. A person whose heart is set on fishing may become angry, frustrated, feel self-pitying, anxious, manipulative, or bitter. Fishing is not sinful, but what a person thinks about it may be.

The following is a list of common idols/lusts with which Christians struggle. Before you read the list, ask God to show you your idols/lusts (Psalm 139:23-24). Circle the ones of which you are guilty.

List of Common Idols ("False Gods") Wives May Have Their Hearts Set On

1. Good health.
2. Physical appearance.
3. Being treated fairly.
4. Having a hurt free/pain free life.
5. Worldly pleasure (drugs, alcohol, sex).
6. Another person (man or woman).

---

[1] Martha Peace, The Excellent Wife: A Biblical Perspective, (Bemidji, MN, Focus Publishing, Inc.,1999) 59-64.

7. A material thing.
8. An ideal ("pro-life movement," "peace movement").
9. Money.
10. Success.
11. Others' approval.
12. Being in control.
13. Having your "needs" met.

As long as things are going well in the areas you have your heart set on, you will feel all right. When they do not turn out as you may desire, frustration and perhaps anxiety begin to build even to the point of desperation. You become willing to do anything, including sin, to have your "idol." In addition to the frustration and possible anxiety, God also frustrates your idol worship because He wants your pure devotion to Him (Matthew 22:37-38). As a result, the painful emotions become seemingly unbearable. Pastor Stuart Scott diagrams what is happening this way:

Pastor Scott's diagram includes a heart which is symbolic of your thoughts, motives, and choices—the "control center" of one's being. The small icons represent what or whom you are worshipping. Your worship is going on every waking moment of every day. You may be worshipping the Lord Jesus Christ or something or someone else.

The small icons represent competing "gods' in our hearts. When something is so important to us that we sin to get it or we sin when it doesn't go well, it can be an idol in our heart.

As idolatrous sin abounds, painful emotions increase, and the pressure builds. It is like a steam engine with no safety or relief valve. If you do not repent and turn to God for a refuge (comfort and relief on His terms), you will be forced to seek relief, comfort, and escape somewhere else. What this amounts to is what David Powlison, from the Christian Counseling and Education Foundation East, calls a "false savior." As you read the following list of "false saviors," think about yourself and circle the ones you have sought for comfort and relief.

List of False Saviors/Refuges

1. Unbiblical view of God ("genie in a bottle obligated to grant your wishes").
2. Sex (immorality, pornography, etc.).
3. Sleep.
4. Work.
5. Television.
6. Reading.
7. Food.

8. Withdrawing, running away.
9. Clinging to people for comfort.
10. Shopping sprees.
11. Sports.
12. Exercise.
13. Recreation.
14. Hobbies.
15. Ministry as an escape.
16. Being busy at church or volunteer activities.
17. Drugs.
18. Alcohol.

Pastor Scott diagrams the release of the pressure in the following way:

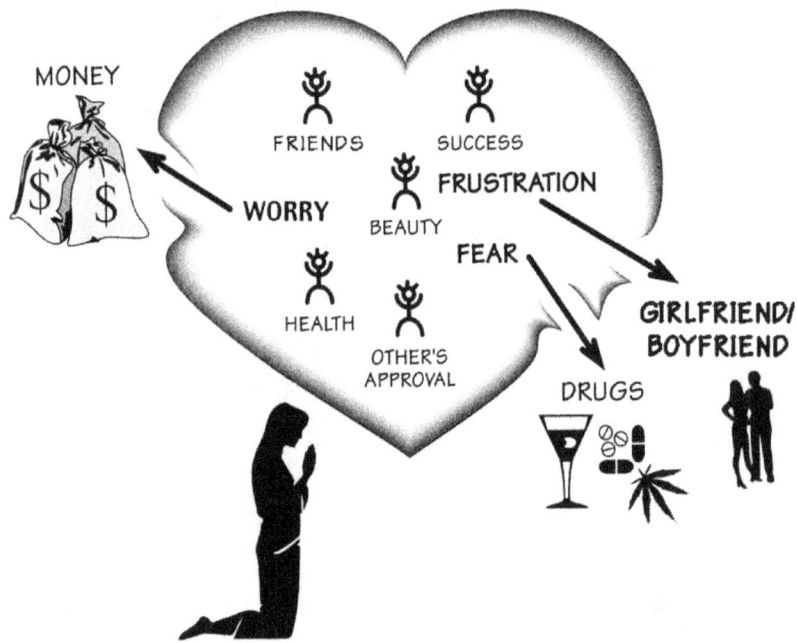

Pursuing a "false savior" only compounds sin and makes matters worse. What may start out as a temporary relief measure may end up enslaving the person and could very well become an idol/lust. Also, there are obvious consequences to seeking such things as food, drugs, or alcohol for relief. Instead of compounding sin, the God of the Bible wants the undivided worship and devotion of your heart. He wants your thoughts, motives, and choices to be focused on glorifying Him. He should be your greatest longing and desire and refuge. Your thoughts, motives, and choices should be set on glorifying Him, not on your idolatrous heart's desires.

Appendix 3: Adoption

(A special thanks to Pastor Bob Bixby of the Morningside Baptist Church, Rockford, IL for writing this essay for inclusion in *Confessions of a Transformed Heart*.)

In his provocative little booklet *The Radical Question: What is Jesus Worth to You?*, David Platt asks, "What if Jesus is worthy of more in our lives than a Christian spin on the American dream?"[1] To *spin* something means to render an interpretation that is favorable to one's personal agenda. Platt's question is accusatory. He is suggesting that Christians in America instinctively know that the American dream is worldly, but they want it. So they put a "Christian spin" on their self-absorbed ambition, and Platt is not buying it. Nor should he. It is spin.

The question is provocative because it exposes our tendency to spin Scripture texts and propositions that call for radical love or care for the poor or self-denial or the supremacy of Jesus in such a way that they lose their finger-pointing harshness and mutate into harmless ditties that coddle our self-congratulatory religion. But Jesus is in fact worthy of more than a token religion that costs little. And devotion for him reduces the American dream into an enemy of the cross that competes for our deepest affections in the secrecy of our private inner-walk with God. The problem is that whether or not there really is a "spin-free zone" in this world, at the judgment seat of Christ there will be no spin at all! We'll have to cope with the bare facts of the Scripture texts and give an account to God for ourselves.

To care for orphans is one such proposition that is hard to avoid and James 1:27 is hard to spin: "Pure and undefiled religion before God and the Father is this: to visit orphans and widows in their trouble, and to keep oneself unspotted from the world."

---

[1] David Platt, *The Radical Question: What is Jesus Worth to You?* (Colorado Springs: Multnomah, 2010), p. 24.

The words *pure* and *undefiled* may seem like an unnecessary redundancy. The word *pure* speaks to the accuracy of one's religion on the external, objective level and the word *undefiled* refers to the authenticity of one's religion on a personal, subjective level. *Pure* was used to speak of that which was ceremonially exact. But we all know that it is possible to be ceremonially exact and doctrinally precise yet unclean in our private thoughts and life. This is what James is referring to when he employs the word *undefiled*. Our religion, the manifestation of our belief through our lifestyle, must be both externally right and internally pure. This point is emphasized by the phrase "before God and the Father." In other words, only the all-knowing God can authenticate our religion as "pure and undefiled." Only God can see the reality of it.

Every Christian who claims to desire a religion that God authenticates should instinctively desire to understand what James is saying about pure and undefiled religion. And one obvious fact leaps out of the verse and demands recognition: there are two qualities of *pure and undefiled religion* that must be evident in a believer's life. Firstly, the believer must "visit orphans and widows in their trouble." And, secondly, believers must keep themselves "unspotted from the world."

To stay "unspotted from the world" is obvious, though not easy. Most believers understand that we are called to be holy, to be separate. Once Jesus saves us from our sins He gives us new affections and a yearning for a heavenly city.

However, it is the phrase about visiting orphans and widows in their trouble that is problematic and uncomfortably inflexible in its wording. It is hard to spin "visit orphans and widows in their trouble" into anything else but exactly what it says. In other words, James is categorically saying that the person who does *not* visit orphans and widows in their trouble *does not have pure and undefiled religion!*

Some may dismiss the obvious implications of the verse because they do not see how they can immediately apply it to their lives. But a sincere Christian must ask, "How does this apply to me?"

It is likely that the phrase *orphans and widows* is used synecdochically. A *synecdoche* is a figure of speech when a part is used to represent the whole. Thus, *orphans and widows* are a representation of the whole of all the various kinds of people that are needy and helpless and in need of mercy. In Bible days, as it is still today in most parts of the world, to be an orphan or a widow was to be in one of the most vulnerable and helpless situations known to society. Thus, *orphans and widows* was shorthand for poor, needy, helpless and vulnerable. No Christian can possibly miss the pain and misery and helplessness of so many people and people groups that exist in his or her sphere of influence today. So even if Christians may not personally know an orphan, they do know of people who meet the description of helpless and needy. They are not exempt from this requirement.

A Christian cannot escape the responsibility of James 1:27 because of the word *visit*. This word is far more than a fifteen-minute drop-in at the retirement home. The word is related to the Greek word *episkopos* from which we get our word *overseer*. We apply that word to the pastor. It is the same word that the Greek translation of the Old Testament used about God coming to the aid of His people. God *visited* His people. He cared for them. He met their needs. He took a pastoral oversight of His people. It implies deliberate and attentive oversight with a commitment to meet whatever needs there may be. In the same way, the Christian who wants a pure and undefiled religion before God must *visit* the helpless and needy.

I would like to suggest a commitment to *visiting* the *orphans* that not only shows pure and undefiled religion, but has the added benefit of providing an excellent means of obeying the Great Commission and modeling the Gospel in real life.

The commitment? Adoption.

The Disciple-making Effect

Every sincere Christian yearns to obey the Great Commission (Matthew 28:19-20) in a real, flesh-and-blood way. Through adoption Christians have to a plan of disciple-making that is one of the most effective known to man: parenting!

Not every one can adopt a child, but I am convinced that more people can do it than realize it and that a Great Commission motivation should highly encourage many in the Church of Jesus Christ to consider adopting an orphan.

The Gospel-Displaying Effect

Every Christian should be excited about the possibility of doing something with his life that displays the glorious truths of the Gospel, the greatest story ever told. And of all the Gospel truths, few are as significant to the believer as the Doctrine of Adoption. Sadly, too many people think of adoption as "Plan B" in family making. But adoption is not "Plan B." When God leads a family to adopt it is "Plan A" for that family.

This is because adoption is God's "Plan A" for making His own family. We who are children of God have been adopted and are in the process of adoption. Our adoption has begun and will culminate when we are finally in heaven.

As the famed Puritan theologian, John Owen, said, "Adoption is the authoritative translation of a believer, by Jesus Christ, from the family of the world and Satan into the family of God, with his investiture in all the privileges and advantages of that family." He called it the "spring and fountain" out of which all of the other blessings we enjoy in Christ flow![2] Joel Beeke explains, "Adoption is what makes sanctification possible and becomes the crowning work of grace in the final analysis. Thus, adoption is both the means by which we enter the family of God and the result of it."[3]

Another theologian, Sinclair Ferguson simplifies John Owen's treatise even more and helps us see how closely the adoption of an orphan into our home resembles the Gospel.

---

[2] John Owen, *Communion with God,* The Works of John Owen, ed. William H. Goold (reprint ed., Edinburgh: Banner of Truth Trust, 1967), 2:207

[3] Joel Beeke, *The Quest for Full Assurance: The Legacy of Calvin and His Successors* (Carlisle: Banner of Truth, 1999), 180.

Adoption

There are five things that occur in an adoption: "(1) the person first belongs to another family; (2) there is a family to which he has no right to belong; (3) there is an authoritative legal translation from one family to another; (4) the adopted person is freed from all the legal obligations of the family from which he came; (5) and by virtue of his translation he is invested with all the rights, privileges, and advantages of the new family."[4]

This is the Gospel! We are all adopted children, and there are few human activities that model the Gospel more effectively than choosing to adopt an orphan and giving him or her the full rights of a family member. Few Christians stop to realize that God could have saved us from our sins without adopting us and giving us all the rights, privileges, and advantages of being in His family as co-heirs with our Elder Brother, Jesus Christ!

The James 1:27 Effect

All Christians should be excited about a practical and effective way they can flesh out James 1:27 in their lifestyles—literally "visiting the orphans" in a show of mercy and Christian love. When a Christian couple adopts they commit themselves to the lifelong "visitation" of an orphan.

Adoption is hard work. It costs. It requires time. Sometimes it is an emotional roller coaster. Adapting to the new life with adoptive parents is often hard for the child and perhaps even disappointing to the adoptive parents. But this is where the rubber meets the road. Adoption takes all of a parent's best "visiting" skills. It requires a deep commitment, but it is one wonderful way a couple and/or family can work together as a team to flesh out pure and undefiled religion.

In conclusion, I would like to say that adoption is usually a tremendous joy and fulfilling delight for the adoptive parents. I do not think that parents should adopt in order to meet their own personal needs as, for example, in seeking to palliate the ache of childlessness. This motive is wrong and too often leads to severe disappointment. Nonetheless, we must not forget that even God

---

[4] Ibid., 180.

adopted us for the sheer delight of owning us and loving us and being a family. In the same way we can rightfully hope that the adoption of a child into our home would be deeply fulfilling and enriching.

As a pastor of many adoptive families and as the father of two adopted children, I have witnessed the deep and lasting joy God gives to both the adoptive families and the adopted children by this wonderful legal transaction. I have had parents of natural born children tell me that the thrill and the joy of having a child by way of adoption was equal to the joy of having a natural born child. One father said that in many ways it is even more thrilling because the entire family committed to the adoption and worked and prayed and gave until it could come to fruition. These families have discovered that adoption is not "Plan B" for making families; it's "Plan A." The families of both natural born and adopted children are providentially one family before God!

Is Jesus worthy of something more in our lives than a Christian spin on the American dream? Dare we actually become radical enough to pursue a pure and undefiled religion? If so, the directives are clear. No one can escape the implications of James 1:27. Our God and adoptive Father expects one kind of religion from us—one that visits the orphans and the widows and that remains spotless from the world.

Perhaps God is not leading you to adopt an orphan, but maybe you can start by praying daily for those who help the orphans. Maybe you can serve the helpless by becoming a foster parent or by helping finance an adoption for a godly Christian family. Whatever you may choose to do, no one can say that there are no orphans to help. No one can say there are no desperately needy. No Christian can dodge James 1:27.

Appendix 4: Discussion Questions

Prologue and Chapter 1: In the Beginning

1. Does a God of love have the right to send us to a place where we are in abject misery? Use Bible characters to support your answer.

Chapter 2: Liberia, Here We Come!

1. What factors did Mark and/or Nancy find especially exciting their first term in missionary service?
2. Was there anything wrong with these good things?

Chapter 3: Rice Riot

1. In retrospect, should Mark and Nancy have anticipated there would be serious political unrest in Liberia?

Chapter 4: An Uncivil War

1. When did the war become especially "real" to Mark and Nancy?
2. Why did the Sheppards think the war would be over when President Doe was killed?

Chapter 5: Refugees

1. Were Mark and Nancy over-confident when they entered refugee work?
2. What factors made refugee work especially difficult for Nancy?
3. Read Appendix 2. Which "idols" was Nancy worshipping? To which false saviors/refuges was she trying to run?

Chapter 6: The Confrontation

1. Why do you think Nancy's friends and family were reluctant to push her to return to refugee work?
2. Do you think either Mark or Nancy fully understood the future ramifications when Mark challenged Nancy to decide

whether or not she could return to refugee work? Can you think of any time in your own life where only in retrospect you realized the importance of a certain moment for you or your family?
3. Mark's conscious effort to please Nancy and her conscious effort to please him increased the love in their marriage. Married women, have you ever made a conscious effort to increase the love you are showing in your marriage?

Chapter 7: Heidi

1. In what ways was Nancy a feminist?
2. Why do some women feel guilty or inadequate if the majority of their time is spent taking care of their own children? What change in thinking can eliminate this faulty view of motherhood?

Chapter 8: Surprised by the Power of Prayer

1. Why was Bloléquin the town in which Nancy least wanted to live? Has God ever asked you to do something that was really difficult?
2. What did God use to display His prayer-answering power to Nancy?
3. To whom does Nancy give credit for her desire to become a woman of prayer? Does this eliminate human responsibility?

Chapter 9: The Emptying

1. What question did Nancy want answered once and for all?
2. After being confronted by God for her pride in its various forms, Nancy had what responsibility? Would it have been enough to simply admit her guilt?
3. Why is it so difficult to give thanks for negative things? Have you ever struggled with obedience to the command, "In everything give thanks"?
4. In what way did Nancy become like Jonah in the Bible? In what way did Nancy become like the 1 Corinthians 13:3 mar-

tyr?
5. What lesson did Nancy learn about love in real life through her interactions with Susanna and Eugene?
6. Why did Nancy say she was an "affirmation junkie"?
7. Why did Mark like it when Nancy quit seeking affirmation?
8. Why had Nancy felt like she was on a hamster wheel during her first term of missionary service?
9. Have you ever experienced God's stripping away of life's treasures so you could find Him?

Chapter 10: In Love

1. Can a person serve God without loving Him?
2. Can a person love God without serving Him?
3. What had Nancy been seeking that in actuality could be found only in God?

Chapter 11: Good News

1. Why did the missionaries call their evangelism program "Operation Andrew"?
2. On whom were the missionaries and church people dependent as they went out to talk to people about Christ? Have you ever been in a similar situation where you realized your total dependency?

Chapter 12: Patience

1. Were Mark and Nancy foolish for taking their children away from the United States and its opportunities?
2. What was Nancy's biggest temptation with home schooling her children? What is your biggest temptation with the children in your life?
3. Why do you think it was important for Nancy to apologize to Nathan as well as to the Lord when she was impatient?

Chapter 13: Mom

1. Why did Mark and Nancy decide to return to Africa despite

her mother's brain tumor?
2. What godly attitude did Nancy's mother display about death?
3. How is the death of a Christian similar to a birth?
4. God provided everything Nancy needed during this difficult time. Have you seen God provide in a special way at the time of a friend or family member's death?

Chapter 14: The Making of a Man
1. Why did Nancy say that Mark was rich and getting richer every day? Have you ever had an opportunity to dramatically increase your own eternal wealth?
2. What good thing happened as a result of the intensity of the assault? Has desperation ever driven you in this same way?
3. Nancy writes that one of the reasons Mark was "the man for this job" was because he had become used to being in trouble as a youth. Have you ever seen God use a weakness, shortcoming or past sin to unexpectedly open up a door of opportunity?

Chapter 15: Becoming Sarah's Daughter
1. What is the difference between submission and reverence?
2. Of what was Nancy afraid? Do you have similar fears?
3. What was the unexpected result of Nancy's increased respect for Mark?
4. Did Mark take this new development for granted, as Nancy had feared? Why or why not?

Chapter 16: Tested by Fire
1. On what subject was the pastor of Karen's church preaching a series of sermons?
2. Why was Karen distraught?
3. What humor did Nancy find in the situation? Why?
4. God worked out the details of a needed house for Nancy and then for Karen. Have you experienced anything similar?
5. What is the key Bible verse for The Treasure Principle? What

does it mean?
6. Do you agree with Nancy that the purifying work God had done in Karen's and her life was the same work He wanted to do in everyone's life?

Chapter 17: Back at Last

1. What was Mark's dream?
2. Why were Mark and Nancy amazed at the timing of their three-week trip into Liberia?

Chapter 18: The Trap Closes

1. Why were foreign citizens being urged to leave Liberia?
2. What factors made Mark's and Nancy's hearts hurt? Have you ever been in a situation where you felt helpless? If so, how did you handle it?

Chapter 19: The Upgrades

1. What was the root of Nancy's jealousy?
2. What load did Mark feel was his to bear and not Nancy's? Have you ever been in a situation where too much information—information that really wasn't for you to know—was the cause of your mental unrest? What, if anything, did you do about it? Have you ever "unloaded" information on someone inappropriately?

Chapter 20: Foolish Things

1. Why did guilt hang over Liberia "like a thick, black cloud"?
2. Was the spiritual condition of Liberia hopeless?
3. What dubious honor did Mark and Nancy have? Have you ever had a similar dubious honor?

Chapter 21: Merri

1. In what condition did Melodie find Mary?
2. Why did Nancy change the spelling of Mary's name to Merri?

3. What evidence did Nancy have that God had changed her heart and taught her to love? Have you ever been pleased to see similar evidence of God's work in your own life?
4. According to Ephesians 1:3-6, what is the Christian's status in God's family?
5. Read Appendix 3. According to James 1:27, what does God say is "pure and undefiled religion"?
6. Do you agree that the "American Dream" is spin?

Chapter 22: Grabbing Grace

1. What does 1 Corinthians 10:13 say God will never allow? Have you ever wondered if He was keeping up His end of the deal?
2. What was the solution to Nancy's dilemma? What are some practical ways to apply that principle in daily life?
3. Nancy was excited to get city electricity. Have you ever seen God provide "grace" in a very practical manner?

Chapter 23: Mouse Poison

1. Why was Mark irritated with Nancy's response to his question about mouse poison? Was his argument valid?
2. Why was Nancy irritated with the question? Was her argument valid?
3. Nancy said she resented being "tweaked" by Mark. Have you ever felt similarly when someone close to you told you of a failure on your part?
4. According to Philippians 2:5-8 Jesus humbled Himself in a number of ways. What are they? Why do we resist humbling ourselves in much lesser ways?
5. Nancy concluded the root of Mark's and her argument was pride. How did she propose it could be avoided the next time?

Chapter 24: Preston

1. What was the relationship between the Sheppard family and

Discussion Questions

   Preston?
2. What was Preston's besetting sin?
3. Do you think Preston ever thought he would be caught and have to face serious consequences? Why or why not? Have you ever been surprised to be caught in your sin?
4. What Bible verses did Nancy stumble across that helped her prepare for the visit to the Ministry of Justice? What prayer?
5. What shock awaited Nancy at the Ministry of Justice? Have you ever been falsely accused?
6. What did Nancy do after the room cleared of the majority of people at the Ministry of Justice? Why?

Epilogue:

1. Nancy says, "It's a biblical paradox: when we choose God we're choosing what's best for us. As a corollary to this, when we choose God we're also choosing what's best for our children." In what ways have you seen this paradox and its corollary played out in your life or the life of someone you know?
2. What have Mark's and Nancy's children gained as a result of their parents' mission work?
3. What has Nancy gained?
4. What "idols" had Nancy been worshipping unknowingly? (See Appendix 2.)
5. Why, according to Nancy, did she flounder when she couldn't see what God was doing?
6 What was Nancy's ultimate conclusion?

Bibliography

Bennett, Arthur (Editor), *The Valley of Vision,* Carlisle, PA, The Banner of Truth Trust, 2005.

Dillow, Linda, *Creative Counterpart: Becoming the Woman, Wife, and Mother You've Longed to Be,* Nashville, TN, Thomas Nelson, Inc., 2003.

Dillow, Linda and Pintus, Lorraine. *Intimate Issues*, Colorado Springs, CO, Waterbrook Press, 1999.

Featherston, William, "My Jesus, I Love Thee," Music: Adoniram Gordon, 1864.

Livingstone, David and Lopez, Faye Springer, "Lord, Send Me Anywhere," Greenville, SC, Musical Ministries / Majesty Music, 1978.

Nicholson, Martha Snell, "Treasures," Chicago, IL, Moody Press, 1952.

Peace, Martha, *The Excellent Wife: A Biblical Perspective*, Bemidji, MN, Focus Publishing, 1999.

Priolo, Lou, *Getting a Grip; The Heart of Anger Handbook for Teens*, Merrick, NY, Calvary Press Publishing, 2006.

Priolo, Lou, *Pleasing People,* Phillipsburg, NJ, P&R Publishing, 2007.

Torrey, R. A., *The Power of Prayer: And the Prayer of Power*, Grand Rapids, MI, Zondervan, 1987

For more information on the Sheppard family's ministry or about other books by Nancy Sheppard, visit their website at www.sheppardsmissions.org

www.ingramcontent.com/pod-product-compliance
Lightning Source LLC
Chambersburg PA
CBHW031348040426
42444CB00005B/224